Mind Body Spirit

The Triple Bond of Optimal Wellness

Keith Karren, PhD

Editorial Staff

Author: Keith Karren, PhD

Executive Editor: Aaron Hardy, MS

Contributing Editor: Kathryn Jenkins

Designer: Integrated Health & Wellness

Integrated Health & Wellness
520 N. Main Street STE C422 | Heber City, UT 84032
Maximizing Human Capital | ihwsolutions.com

ISBN: 978-0-692-92127-2
©2018 Keith Karren, PhD (Written Content)
©2018 Integrated Health & Wellness (Design & Layout)
Information may not be reproduced, copied, cited, or
circulated in any printed or electronic form without written
permission from Integrated Health & Wellness.

This publication is based on research and is based on the knowledge and ideas of the author. The purpose of this publication is to provide helpful information for the health of it's readers. It is sold with the understanding that the author and publisher are not engaged in rendering health, medical, or other professional advice to the individual reader. The reader should not use the information contained in this publication as a substitute for the advice of a licensed health care professional.

Table of Contents

Introduction

Redesigning Your Life through Mind-Body-Spirit Balance

mindset
balance care
positive chakra sleep
body attitude emotions
training health vitality fun
recreation diet quality of life fitness
optimism rest therapy
mind
fun spiritual feelings
massage healthcare education
purpose exercise wellness
care

What is wellness?

Introduction
Redesigning Your Life through Mind-Body-Spirit Balance

Health is a large word. It embraces not the body only, but the mind and spirit as well; . . . and not today's pain or pleasure alone, but the whole being and outlook of a man.
James H. West, internist

If you think a well-toned, properly fueled body is the key to wellness, you're right. Well, to be more exact, you're only a third right - because optimum wellness involves not just your body, but a solid balance between your mind, your body, and your spirit.

It all boils down to *psychoneuroendocrineimmunology*. That's quite a mouthful - and chances are good that you've never tried to wrap your tongue around it before right now. Let's make it simple: it's a science that shows how your mind, body, and spirit are all linked together and how they help you resist disease and infection. And it might sound like a bunch of hocus-pocus, but some of the nation's leading researchers and medical experts have put their enthusiastic stamp of approval on it.

In fact, researchers at Harvard Medical School and the California Pacific Medical Center had this to say: there is now "considerable evidence" that boosting up traditional treatment by addressing the mind and spirit in addition to the body can be "effective" in treating a number of conditions. That includes stuff as diverse as cancer and heart disease to things like chronic low back pain, insomnia, headache, and depression.

Researchers and doctors all over the world have been finding success with mind-body-spirit therapies. It's pretty exciting: as just one example, they've shown how changing up emotions can make a big difference in diabetes and improves things like cholesterol, glucose levels, heart rate, and blood pressure. They've also found that meditation dramatically impacts chronic pain, anxiety, and depression, in addition to bringing on positive changes in the brain.

And that's not even the tip of the iceberg. But before we let you in on all that, we need to set the stage for some very revolutionary ideas we're about to share. And to do that, let's start at the very beginning.

Wellness. It's a word you hear all the time; you've probably even used it yourself. But what exactly is it? Wellness is a sense of well-being that results from the good health of a balanced body, mind, and spirit. To put it simply, we are a spirit, we have a mind, and we live in a body. They're all connected. And if we want to experience wellness, all three must be balanced. When that balance exists, your immune system is stronger, and you're better able to fend off infection and disease. Here's the best part of all: even if your body isn't perfect, you can still enjoy wellness.

Let's briefly look at those three components. Your **body**, of course, is made up of biochemical cells, organs, and systems that are engineered in part by your DNA, or your genetics. It's all laced together by a fantastic network of nerves and blood vessels. It includes your five senses and all the physical factors that allow you to express yourself. Running the whole show is your brain, a complex sweatshop that does everything from solving problems to making sure your heart keeps beating and your stomach keeps digesting your food. The most incredible computer system on the planet pales in comparison to what the brain can do.

Balancing is the key to create an extraordinary life.

Your **mind** brings an amazing amount to the table. Your mind is different from your brain, which is a physical organ. Your mind includes your attitudes, emotions, feelings, memories, and judgment. Your mind gives you the ability to think, reason, and make choices. Your mind interprets the experiences you have every day from the time you wake up until you drift back to sleep at night - and determines whether you experience stress, joy, anxiety, elation, depression, fright, or calm in response to what's happening around you.

Finally, your **spirit** is what gives your life meaning and purpose. It fashions your inner beliefs and yearns for inspiration. Through your spirit you experience love, bond with family and friends, connect to divinity, identify a unique mission in your life, find the motivation to serve others, and practice religious belief.

Here's just one simple example of how the mind, body, and spirit are linked. You're at the park sitting on a bench while you watch your toddler - a little boy with a mop of curly brown hair and an endless supply of energy who has totally captured your heart (a manifestation of your spirit). You look down for just a few minutes to answer a text, and when you look up, you can't see him anywhere. He has vanished into thin air - or so it seems.

Your mind immediately leaps to all the worst scenarios. You instantly recall last night's episode of *Law and Order: Special Victims Unit* while fear clutches you in its iron grip. And without even a flicker of a conscious effort on your part, your body flies into action in response to that fear, flooding your system with adrenalin, razor-sharp vision, and increased blood flow to your legs - all of which allow you to start running all over that park in search of your little boy.

That's a simple example, but it's just one of countless ways in which our magnificent minds, bodies, and spirits are connected.

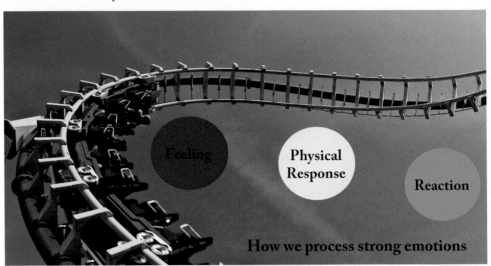

So how did somebody first manage to connect all the dots? Well, it wasn't exactly in our day and age. Most ancient healing practices operated on the belief that the mind and body were robustly linked - it was Western medicine that was convinced the two were completely separate. Simply put, we lagged way behind when it came to the kind of enlightened thinking required to figure it all out.

All that started to change in 1964 when a psychiatrist named George Solomon noticed something strange: people who had rheumatoid arthritis - an autoimmune disorder, or form of arthritis impacted by the immune system - were consistently worse when they were depressed. Following up on his observations, he started in earnest to study the impact of emotions on inflammation and the immune system in general. The new field was called *psychoneuroimmunology* (*psycho* for the mind, *neuro* for the nervous system, and immunology for the immune system).

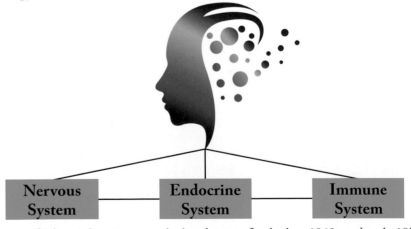

Others were fairly quick to jump on the bandwagon. In the late 1960s and early 1970s, cardiologist Herbert Benson figured out that intense emotions and feelings sent blood pressure skyrocketing - and that meditation brought it back down to earth. He coined the term relaxation response to describe his findings. And in 1975, psychologist Robert Ader identified a host of emotional and mental cues that affected the immune system.

Western scientists and physicians realized they were on to something big. Experiment after experiment showed that emotions (produced by the mind) and beliefs (connected to the spirit) have a dramatic effect on the immune system (part of the body). That led to experiments demonstrating that the immune system can even be trained. (Think Pavlov's dogs here.) One classic involved mice - researchers gave mice saccharin along with a drug that suppressed the immune system. The drug caused nausea, made the mice act sick, and sometimes even killed them. Then the scientists took away the drug. The mice were given pure saccharin. What happened? The mice reacted just like they did when they got the immune-suppressing drug: they got sick. Some even died. From saccharin. Confronted with the taste of saccharin, their immune systems had come to expect the harmful drug, and they responded exactly as they had to the drug.

Finally, Harvard University researcher Candace Pert found that every emotion we experience causes the body to create a chain of molecules. Her pioneering research and that of others who followed found that positive emotions and the positive experiences linked to them - love, altruism, forgiveness, strong social support, humor, healthy marriages, optimism, hope, laughter, prayer, strong families, and regular participation in worship services, among them - produce the molecules that boost the immune system and protect against disease.

You guessed it: negative emotions do exactly the opposite. Anger and hostility are among the worst, packing a punch that rips up the linings of the blood vessels. Among the other culprits are hatred, jealously, revenge, isolation, anxiety, worry, depression, pessimism, and stress. Nurse them along for too long, and they batter your immune system and render you less able to fight off infection or disease. In fact, at their extreme, they make you more susceptible to disease. They become disease magnets.

Research continues. Scientist have verified that all the organs of the body and all the emotions we experience share the same chemical language and are constantly communicating with each other. No piece is an island, so to say. And the loudest voice of all may be the immune system. Researchers recently found that intense emotions like rage, fear, and anger not only hurt the immune system but lead to stress, which causes the body to release epinephrine. Epinephrine causes a chemical breakdown that weakens the immune system and renders you susceptible to illness and disease. It's one of the most vicious cycles we know.

The secret of health for both mind and body is not to mourn for the past, not to worry about the future, or not to anticipate troubles, but to live the present moment wisely and earnestly.

Siddarth Guatama
Buddha

And try on these study results for size: It's long been known that people who exercise are healthier. Now researchers are starting to sort out why, and it goes far beyond increased blood circulation or working out the muscles. Here's what's really happening: as any regular jogger can tell you, exercise improves mental state. And an improved mental state boosts immunity. And increased immunity makes you healthier. Another example of connecting the dots - and the total opposite of a vicious cycle.

Exercise Benefits:

Reduced anxiety and depression

Stress reliever

Promotes positive mood

Increase of self-esteem

Better sleep pattern

Increased social confidence

Distraction

Lots of what we know has originally taken place in laboratories. How about an example of how it impacts you in your everyday life? Here's a good one: Let's say you're exposed to any of a hundred viruses that cause the common cold. Your body normally launches what's known as the sickness response. You probably know it well: you get a fever, feel a bit anxious, seem to be wiped out, no longer really want to eat or drink (or have sex, for that matter), get a scratchy throat, and start to ache. There's no question about it: you're sick.

Through a complex set of responses, the virus hooks up with your immune system to tell your brain that you're sick. Your brain responds with a cascade of symptoms that include the ones listed above.

Researchers have now found that you can experience every one of those same symptoms without being exposed to a cold virus at all. Instead of the virus telling your brain that you're sick, your brain - triggered by stress or another intense emotion - convinces your body that you're sick. And your body believes every bit of it. Again, there's no question about it: you're sick. Only this time, you're not contagious.

We'll go into more detail on all of this later. For now, trust us.

In the meantime, here's the exciting part of everything we've packed between the covers of this book: To a large extent, you are in control. While you can't change what you inherited from your parents, you can determine how you will use your mind and your spirit in positive, health-centered ways to improve immunity and physical well-being. You can engage your thoughts, emotions, perceptions, and choices in a way that will ease your pain, manage any illness, and help you feel physically great.

You can try out techniques like cognitive behavioral therapy, biofeedback, stress management, meditation, or other relaxation procedures to improve the way you feel and function. And don't be surprised if your doctor suggests some of these along with traditional medical treatments for maladies like cancer, high blood pressure, asthma, heart disease, diabetes, insomnia, fibromyalgia, chronic pain, Crohn's disease, depression, or a whole rainbow of other disorders.

But most simple of all, you can give your emotions a tune-up. You can change the way you look at things, improve your perceptions. You just might find that you're feeling stronger and more energetic in the bargain.

So start reading - and then start doing! As Dr. Fabrizio Mancini wrote, "The greatest miracle on Earth is the human body. It is stronger and wiser than you may realize, and improving its ability to self-heal is within your control." Ready to start on that amazing journey?

Just turn the page!

Your happiness is in your hands.

You are in charge of you.

Today, what did I do for my mind, my body, my spirit?

My relationships, my creativity and my passions?

Chapter 1

The Connection between Mind and Body

MIND

Chapter 1
The Connection between Mind and Body

The root of all health is in the brain.
The trunk of it is in emotion. The branches and the
leaves are the body. The flower of health blooms
when all parts work together.
Kurdish folk saying

Want to live longer - especially in the blush of good health? Who doesn't, right? Well, before you order the latest elixir advertised on the Internet or get sucked into one of those kiosks in the mall, take a good, hard look at yourself. Because, as the Kurdish folk saying above so beautifully puts it, all the things you need to live longer and better are right within your reach. They're not available at any pharmacy, and you don't have to go out and buy them. You were born with them.

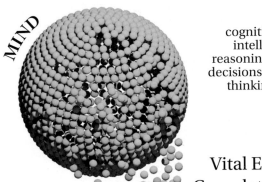

MIND

cognitive faculties, brain, logic, thoughts, intellect, beliefs, conscious, judgment, reasoning, attitudes, will, choices, reasonings, decisions, emotions, self-talk, response, critical thinking, memory linear time, emotions, protection, planning.

Vital Elements to Complete Well-Being

physical body composition, skin, bones, nervous system, fat, organs, muscles, blood, brain, bacteria, neurons, endocrine glands, average 75 trillion cells, immune system.

BODY

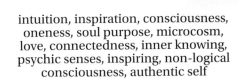

SPIRIT

intuition, inspiration, consciousness, oneness, soul purpose, microcosm, love, connectedness, inner knowing, psychic senses, inspiring, non-logical consciousness, authentic self

14

In the Introduction, we acquainted you with *psychoneuroendocrineimmunology*. Big word. Even bigger concept. Remember? It's a science (no questionable potions here) that shows how your mind, body, and spirit are all linked together. Even better, it shows how your mind, body, and spirit work together to keep you healthy to resist disease and infection. And the frosting on the cake is that they also help you live longer.

If that sounds far-fetched, think about this: one well-respected doctor estimated that 90 percent of all the diseases he treats have emotional roots - and he actually thought that estimate was conservative. And while "modern" medicine has just been catching up to that notion in the last few decades, physicians have actually known and written about the links between the mind, body, and spirit for centuries. Solid research and respected science is now telling us what all those practitioners knew long before there were planes, trains, and automobiles: Our state of mind and emotions directly impact our physical health - for good or for bad.

We actually have a leg up on the practitioners from centuries ago: what they intuitively "knew" we can now prove through advances in molecular biology and neuroscience. Simply put, we now have the scientific ability and instruments to follow even the most microscopic cells through the body and to watch how those cells act and are acted on. Scientists are looking at how the body communicates with the immune system and how it communicates back again as well as what role the mind and emotions have in the whole process. That determines how and why we get sick, and the findings are going to transform what we do to stay well. These same scientists are also looking at exactly how the mind and spirit enter into the picture, because there's no doubt that they are major players.

Armies of researchers are conducting ongoing research, and the results - ideas that seem revolutionary to us now - will be commonplace in classrooms by the time today's kindergarteners reach high school . . . if not before. We're not going to give you the scientific details in this book, but we are going to share enough so you can take charge of your own health and reap the benefits - benefits like a good, long life.

What they're doing in labs throughout the world is pretty much rocket science. But here's the good news: Once you know a few basics, you won't need rocket science to protect your health and boost your longevity!

Let's start by looking at the various dimensions of health and how they work together to keep you well and prolong your life.

The Five Dimensions of Health

If you're like most other people, when you hear the word health, you immediately think of the physical body - and whether yours is in great shape. There's no doubt about it: physical health is important, but it's only part of the picture.

In 1948, the World Health Organization (WHO) identified five dimensions that, together, determine how healthy you are. These parameters were so sound that they still serve as the benchmark for assessing overall health today. The quality of your life and your anticipated longevity depend on how balanced these dimensions are and the ways in which they interact.

The greatest mistake in the treatment of diseases is that there are physicians for the body and physicians for the soul, although the two cannot be separated.

Plato

We'll start with the most obvious dimension - physical health - and move on to some others to which you may not have given a lot of thought.

Physical Health

As its name implies, physical health has to do with the health of the body and its ability to perform the functions essential to well-being. These include the things you think about - climbing stairs, running on a treadmill, writing on a chalkboard - as well as the things your body does without you even being aware of them, such as keeping your heart beating and digesting your food and maintaining your body temperature.

Established numbers help determine whether physical health is at its optimum; your doctor, nutritional coach, or trainer can provide you with optimum indicators for weight, blood pressure, blood sugar, and body mass index (BMI). Pay attention to those and consider adjustments if necessary.

Things you can do to boost physical health

- Eat healthy, nutritious food
- Drink plenty of water
- Don't skip meals; breakfast is especially important
- Cut back on sugar and salt
- Get enough sleep; seven hours a night is considered optimal
- Exercise regularly to stay in shape and to build immunity
- Avoid addictive substances and recreational drugs
- Get regular physical exams
- See a doctor if you develop symptoms
- Don't overuse or misuse prescription medications

Physical health impacts the other dimensions of health in a number of ways. For example, eating nutrient-dense food not only keeps your body healthy and strong, but it energizes your mind and helps you think clearly. Your goal for physical health is to build stamina, endurance, and flexibility and to help you maintain a physical condition that lets you meet personal and workplace demands without difficulty.

Emotional Health

Your emotions encompass a number of things, including your attitude and your feelings - things like love, joy, fear, hope, anger, happiness, frustration, eagerness, sadness, or stress. Everyone occasionally experiences both positive and negative emotions, and emotional health determines your ability to acknowledge your feelings and cope with emotions of all kinds. The way in which you respond to both positive and negative situations is a good indicator of your emotional health.

One of the most important facets of emotional health is to be in tune with your feelings and to take the steps necessary to address any difficulties. Everyone has occasional disappointments or even really hard times; emotional well-being enables you to keep a positive outlook and move forward with hope despite these types of setbacks.

Things you can do to improve emotional health

- Look for the positive, both overall and in particular situations
- Be aware of your strengths, weaknesses, and limitations
- Learn to express yourself appropriately
- Set priorities and address top priorities first
- Share your feelings, even those that are difficult
- Learn to manage stress effectively
- Build strong networks with family, friends, peers, and students
- Tune into your feelings

Have a positive attitude, high self-esteem, a strong sense of self, and the ability to recognize and share a wide range of feelings with others in a constructive way.

Research has shown that all kinds of emotions have direct impact on physical health. For example, anger and hostility literally corrode the linings of the blood vessels and dramatically increase the risk of cardiovascular disease. Burying emotions instead of acknowledging and appropriately expressing them has been shown to increase the risk of heart disease and cancer. And stress wreaks all kinds of havoc on the body; for one thing, it causes the body to produce hormones that are harmful to the heart and that deal a powerful punch to the immune system, making it more difficult to resist disease or heal if you do get sick.

Intellectual Health

Intellectual well-being allows you to engage others and actively participate in the world around you. Strong intellectual health helps you acquire the knowledge and skills you need to advance in your career and to enjoy your personal life. It also contributes to your ability to solve problems and arrive at creative ways to approach difficulties you encounter (and we *all* encounter them!).

Be open to new ideas, be creative, think critically, and seek out new challenges.

You are better able to accept new ways of doing things, evaluate potential solutions, and adopt new ideas when you have good intellectual well-being. Intellectual health is also what enables you to become absorbed in creative and stimulating activities that bring meaning and fun to life. Many also enjoy a great deal of growth by being open to exploration and new discoveries that then lead to new insights.

Intellectual health doesn't necessarily mean capturing a high grade-point average or knowing all the answers on Jeopardy! It has much more to do with being curious and open to new adventures.

Things you can do to improve intellectual health

- Approach new opportunities with an open mind
- Take advantage of the chance to learn new things
- Actively seek challenges
- Set challenging but realistic goals
- Seek stimulation and mental growth
- Get involved in cultural experiences
- Bring new ideas and methods to the table
- Never stop learning

Intellectual health requires a clear, active mind that can efficiently process and interpret information from all its various sources. Good physical health and the food that fuels it helps keep your brain functioning and provides the foundation for intellectual wellness.

Social Health

Good social health enables us to build and maintain healthy relationships with those important to us - family members, friends, peers, and students. Social wellness enables you to respect yourself and others, set reasonable and healthy boundaries, and establish meaningful connections with other people. Building good communication skills is part of social health and is basic to the ability to maintain good relationships.

As social beings, it's important to us to be accepted by others and to feel comfortable in relating to people around us. Those with good social health are at ease with others, actively seek out companionship, work to contribute to relationships, and build strong social networks through which they can both give and take benefits of being with others.

Things you can do to improve social health

- Improve your ability to interact with other people
- Build your own self-image so you feel comfortable among others
- Be receptive to the ideas and experiences of others
- Use empathy to help you understand others
- Build networks among diverse types of people
- Seek to make new friends and establish new professional contacts
- Work to understand various cultural norms
- Become committed to the common welfare of your school or community

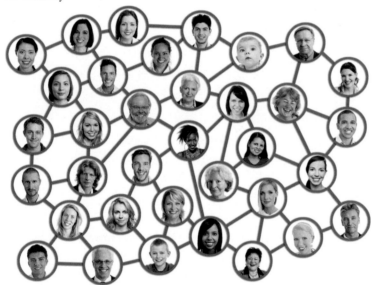

Don't chase people. Be yourself, do your own thing and work hard. The right people – the ones who really belong in your life – will come to you. And stay.

Will Smith

The lyrics of a song popular in the seventies said that "people who need people are the luckiest people in the world." Research has shown that they are also the healthiest people in the world. Scientists have shown that a strong social network and good relationships with friends and family boosts health and strengthens the immune system, making you much better able to resist disease. Research involving a group of Italian immigrants in Pennsylvania determined that they owed their robust heart health to their active social ties.

In contrast, studies have found that isolation and weak social ties are high risk factors for poor physical and mental health.

Spiritual Health

Spiritual health - what some consider to be the heart of mind-body medicine - has little to do with church participation or membership. Rather, it is your ability to have and understand a real purpose in life; strong spiritual health results when you have a set of personal values and beliefs that guide your decisions, behavior, and goals. Spirituality involves our innate ability to love, feel compassion, and experience joy. Spiritual well-being helps you live in harmony with yourself and others and forms your goals and aspirations, regardless of whether you belong and participate in a specific religion. While many find spirituality through religion, others find it through things like nature, art, music, or uplifting literature.

Find meaning in life events, demonstrate individual purposes, and live a life that reflects your values and beliefs.

Of all the dimensions of wellness, the spiritual dimension is by far the most intimate and personal. It requires you to call on things that are deep within your soul and involves your understanding of and relationship to your God, Creator, or Higher Power. In large part, the activities connected to the spiritual dimension of health call on your ability to see deep within yourself so that your beliefs, values, and behavior are congruent.

A healthy spiritual life is one in which you are loving and tolerant of others and sincerely strive to live in harmony with yourself and others. It is the way through which you find comfort, hope, meaning, and inner peace in your life.

Things you can do to improve spiritual health

- Make sure your actions and decisions are consistent with your values
- Be tolerant of the views of others
- Spend time thinking about your purpose in life
- Set aside time each day to do those things that increase your spirituality - pray, meditate, take a walk in nature, listen to beautiful music, or do volunteer work, for example
- Spend time each day just being quiet or relaxing and thinking outside yourself

At the still point of the turning world, there the dance is.

T. S. Eliot

Studies show that those who have well-defined spiritual beliefs that guide their behavior and decisions are consistently in better physical and mental health and enjoy stronger immunity. They have also been shown to better manage stress, which contributes to better physical, mental, and social health.

Of the five dimensions of health defined by the WHO, spiritual health is the one that is most intensely personal - and, as a result, is also the one most difficult to define and prescribe. That having been said, it is also one of the most important dimensions of health, contributing to an ultimate sense of happiness.

The five dimensions of health are much like a jigsaw puzzle: each interlocking dimension fits with the others to form a complete picture of health and well-being. If you're missing a piece - one of the crucial dimensions - the picture will be incomplete, will be unbalanced, and will lack sense and meaning.

Two Other Dimensions

In the more than six decades since the WHO introduced the five dimensions of health, some have suggested that there are two additional dimensions that should be considered and addressed in a discussion of wellness. Those dimensions are occupational wellness and environmental wellness.

Occupational Wellness

Occupational wellness describes the ability to find fulfillment and creative energy in the work you do. It also pertains to your ability to manage stress on the job, to balance your work and personal lives in a way that brings enjoyment from both, and to make a positive impact in the school, in the community, and in the lives of your students.

People employed in a full-time position spend more hours at work than they do at home with their families or in any other pursuit in life - so it's important to pursue something you enjoy as an occupation. If you find yourself getting burned out or losing the joy you once found in what you're doing, you might consider exploring other options in education, perhaps in an administrative or research capacity.

Things you can do to improve occupational health

- Talk openly with your administrator and coworkers
- Do things that help you enjoy your job
- When an occasional "bad day" happens, focus on the positive
- Regularly assess your workload to make sure that what you've been asked to do won't overload you or burn you out
- Schedule in time each day to do something fun or to relax

Seek to have a career that is interesting, enjoyable, meaningful and that contributes to the larger society.

Environmental Wellness

Every person in the world shares something in common with every other member of the global community: we all live on this earth and share responsibility and stewardship over it. The environmental dimension of health calls on all of us to help maintain the quality of the air, water, and land on this planet. That obligation starts in our homes and extends to our communities.

Be aware of the interactions between the environment, community and yourself and behave in ways that care for each of these responsibly.

We can exercise environmental wellness by having a positive impact on the environment and by making sure that we teach others what needs to be done to discharge our shared responsibility.

Things you can do to improve environmental health

- Educate yourself about what can be done to safeguard the environment in the area where you live
- Teach family members and students how they can help
- Avoid doing things that would have a negative impact on the air, water, or land
- Become cognizant of how your daily habits affect the environment and make any changes that are necessary
- Protect yourself from environmental hazards
- Help others be aware of the earth's specific resources and limitations

Mind, Body, Spirit: Always Talking

You may not have spent a lot of time thinking about the way your body works. You just know that it works, and you probably haven't worried much about what actually goes on in there. That's how it is with most people - until they get sick. Then, suddenly, it's time to sit up and take notice.

And that's not all: most people think that whatever is going on in there has to do with

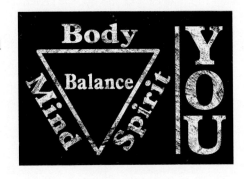

stomachs or hearts or that little accessory wad of tissue called an appendix, with a few bacteria or viruses thrown into the mix for good measure. Well, that's just the tip of the iceberg, and if that's all you attend to, chances are you're missing out on the very things that can help you get and stay well.

Because there's a whole lot of high-level communication going on in your body, not just between your major organs and systems but between the things that comprise your body, your mind, your emotions, and your spirit. Scientists have discovered that every time you experience an emotion - any emotion, good or bad - your body responds by producing chains of molecules. Those chains of molecules have real, physical, chemical effects on your body, good or bad. Examples? Anger beats up your cardiovascular system. Stress knocks out your immune system. Optimism does all sorts of good things to your body.

The Neuro, Endo, and Immune systems are in constant conversation.

Here's just a teaser to get you thinking in the right direction: What would you say if you knew you could be exposed to the most vicious cold virus in the world and you wouldn't get sick?

It can happen, and does happen all the time. Research has proved it. Numerous studies show that people with a good sense of humor, the ones who see the comical in things, got far fewer colds. In another study, researchers showed men an hour-long humorous video; markers in their immune systems increased and stayed stronger for as long as twelve hours afterward. And in many studies, people who laugh are physically healthier in all kinds of ways. And that's no laughing matter: Researchers have concluded that something about humor and laughter literally turns on the immune system, keeping your body in better health.

The opposite happens, too. There's an antibody in your saliva, S-IgA, that protects you from the common cold. Remember the funny video effect on the immune system? Well, the opposite held true in another study, where volunteers looked at pictures and watched videos intended to make them angry. Once they were angry, the levels of S-IgA in their saliva was significantly reduced for as long as  five hours, making them more susceptible to the common cold. In other studies, students under stress had significantly less S-IgA in their saliva and got lots more colds as well as other infectious diseases. So did the students with few friends; the ones who had a strong social network virtually pumped out the S-IgA and stayed far healthier.

Or think about this: depression and stress both knock out immunity in lots of ways. We'll talk about stress in greater detail in the next chapter, but for now, let's just skim the surface. British researchers asked people questions to determine how depressed or stressed they were. Then they exposed all the people in the study to a tiny amount of cold virus in some nose drops. You guessed it: the stressed, depressed people got colds at a *much* higher rate than those who didn't feel that way.

Here's another example: Research at Virginia Tech in Blacksburg, Virginia, studied students who had a pessimistic outlook on life. It found that those students went to the doctor four times as often as the optimistic students for physical illnesses - 95 percent of the time with infectious diseases, most often the common cold.

How does it happen? Simply, the major body systems, the mind, the emotions, and the immune system - that finely tuned system that protects you from disease and helps you heal - have a complex, intricate dialogue going on all the time, even if you've never heard it.

As our feelings change, this mixture of peptides travels throughout your body and your brain. And they're literally changing the chemistry of every cell in your body.

Dr. Candace Pert

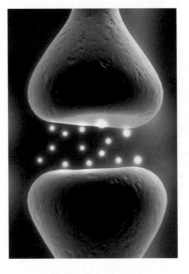

Stress, particularly chronic stress, wreaks havoc on your body. Negative emotions - anger, hostility, depression, despair, fear, anxiety, grief, and pessimism, among them - cripple immunity and work like heat-seeking missiles to hurt specific organs and systems. Positive emotions, such as love and joy and happiness, boost immunity and help protect health.

Obviously, there's some pretty impressive communication going on between the emotions and the body. So where does the mind come in? Consider the brain: a relatively puny organ that makes up only about 2 percent of your body's weight needs about 25 percent of your body's nutrients - stuff like water, vitamins, minerals, essential fatty acids, complex carbohydrates, and amino acids - in order to stay in top form.

What's going on in your brain determines not only what goes on in your mind, but what goes on in your body. Billions of nerve cells laced throughout the brain let it communicate with itself, but also enable it to communicate with all other parts of the body, including the immune system. What you think travels throughout your body along networks of nerves that make the most sophisticated computer or telecommunications networks look primitive.

The body sends its share of information back to the brain along those same networks of nerves in an impressive exchange. We're learning more every day about how this works and what the effects are. As just one example, so many nerves send out impulses from the digestive system that it has become known as "the second brain." In fact, a stunning 95 percent of the body's serotonin (the "feel good" hormone) and neurotransmitters *originate* in the gastrointestinal tract. The connection between the body and the mind can no longer be disputed.

So where does the spirit enter into the picture? The nurturing of spiritual health has been shown to have a dramatic influence on both physical and mental health. That could be because many of the aspects of spiritual health - faith, hope, commitment, enhanced self-esteem, a sense of control, a sense of purpose, and strong connections with others - are the same factors that protect health and boost immunity.

Research done at UCLA found that spiritual practices, including things like prayer and meditation, literally reduce pain by increasing the secretion of hormones that reduce pain, among them serotonin and norepinephrine. Did you get that? The things you do to enhance your spiritual health actually cause the body to secrete more of the hormones that reduce pain.

You've certainly heard (and possibly even taught) the jingle that proclaims, "The hip bone's connected to the thigh bone." When it comes to your body, mind, and spirit, the connections are powerful and beyond any doubt. Those are the things that are *really* connected.

How the Mind and Spirit Affect Longevity

We started this chapter by asking who wouldn't want to live longer. You've probably heard a lot about the physical things you can do to tack a few extra years onto your life: Eat right. Exercise regularly. Get enough sleep. Don't smoke. Fasten your seatbelt every time you get in the car. Avoid noxious pollutants. Don't take unnecessary risks. And inherit some good, strong DNA.

But did you ever think that the way you think has a lot to do with your lifespan?

Well, it does. By this point, it shouldn't surprise you that your mind and your spirit join hands with your body in determining how long you will live.

One landmark study in Sweden looked at people in a major city, eight smaller towns, and a number of small communities and villages. Each person in the study got a thorough medical exam, a psychological assessment, and an examination of sociological data (measuring things like the strength of their social network, the condition of their housing, their education, their income, and so on). They were also interviewed in depth about the quality of their lives.

The findings pointed to a powerful link between the body, the mind, and the spirit in how long people are likely to live.

The Swedish study showed that the people who lived to the age of one hundred or older had some definite physical things in common. They had great genetics; they had parents, grandparents, and great-grandparents who lived long lives. Two other powerful physical factors were body composition and blood pressure. In addition, most had never smoked.

Facts about Mind-Body-Spirit Health

- Every one of us is a combination of a mind, a body, and a spirit, and all three influence our health.
- The nervous, immune, and endocrine systems "talk" to each other and take their direction from the mind.
- Negative emotions such as worry, anxiety, depression, hostility, and anger, when nurtured, can increase susceptibility to disease
- Anger and hostility are more damaging to the heart that a high-fat diet.
- Virtually every illness is influenced for good or bad by the way we feel and think.
- Every thought and spiritual feeling sets off a cascade of cellular reactions that impact every molecule in the body.
- Stress is linked to a wide variety of health problems.
- The mind, body, and spirit are interdependent, so taking care of each one affects the other two.
- People with good social support live longer and have better health.
- Altruism, the act of giving of yourself out of genuine concern for others, is one of the healthiest of all attributes.
- We have an amazing potential to heal and transform ourselves through our thoughts, perceptions, and choices. Much of what we are is up to us.

But the mind and spirit had a definite impact as well. The longest-living people were relaxed, easygoing, less prone to anxiety, and emotionally stable. They were also responsible and capable. Spiritually, they had a strong purpose in life and a high quality of life. They tended to have strong marriages and families; only 2 percent had ever divorced, and only 19 percent had never married.

The positive impact of the mind on longevity seems to be related to the mind's effect on the immune system. There are many events associated with old age that impair immunity: at around age sixty and progressively after that, the various cells of the immune system decline in number and effectiveness. It's just a fact of life. That's not all: the life events associated with old age - retirement, loss of significant others, economic stress, reduction in mobility, poor nutrition, physical disability, bereavement, loneliness or isolation, and a less active role in society, among them - are also things that are known to reduce immunity. But remember: those things can be compensated for by positively adapting, coping with changes, and pursuing the mental, physical, and spiritual things we know to improve immunity and protect health.

What it all means is this: positive physical, mental, social, emotional, and spiritual things are important to you no matter how old you are. They become even more important as you age.

Integrative Medicine, Good Health, and Long Life

Obviously, countless eager scientists the world over are busily researching how the mind, body, and spirit work together to protect health and result in long life.

But let's face it: all the research in the world isn't going to help unless someone starts translating that research into *treatment*. And let's also face another important fact: just because you're now learning about all the ways in which your mind, body, and spirit work together doesn't mean you can take a quick do-it-yourself course and have all your problems licked.

Luckily, a group of dedicated practitioners are taking everything the researchers are learning and putting together a revolutionary new kind of treatment called *integrative medicine*. They're making it work. And best of all, you're not left on your own to figure it all out.

What's integrative medicine? Basically, it's a practice of medicine that goes far beyond the traditional approach of treating the body. Integrative medicine combines mainstream medical therapies with the best and most validated therapies from each type of medicine, focusing on practices that have high-quality evidence of safety and effectiveness. It has gained so much favor that there's actually a division of the National Institutes of Health that is devoted to it.

Dr. Andrew Weil, a pioneer of integrative medicine, explains the philosophies that make this practice of medicine so different. Chief among those is a partnership between the patient and the practitioner and the recognition that good medicine is based on solid science, is open to new ideas, and is driven by inquiry. Integrative medicine is dedicated to the appropriate use of both conventional and alternative methods to achieve healing and a consideration of all factors that could work together to both cause and heal illness, including the mind, body, and spirit.

Dr. Weil points out that integrative medicine is dedicated to the use of effective, less invasive treatment whenever possible and focuses on treatment of the *whole* person - not just the body, but the mind and spirit as well. The main goal of integrative medicine is to preserve health and prevent disease, not just to treat disease when it happens.

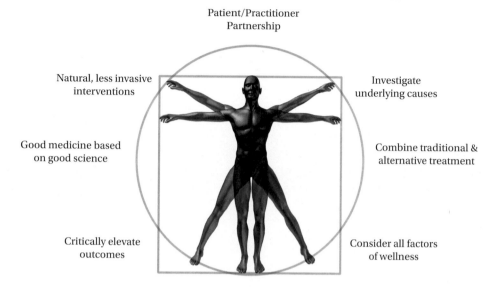

Integrative medicine is gaining popularity and acceptance throughout the medical community. The number of American hospitals that use some form of integrative medicine has more than doubled in the last decade. It's being adopted in unprecedented numbers in clinics and physicians' offices, and it's being taught in an increasing number of medical schools. According to the *Journal of the American Medical Association*, more Americans are now going to practitioners of integrative medicine than are visiting conventional physicians. In a national survey, 38 percent of all Americans were drawn to integrative medicine.

Maybe it's time for you to hop on board if you haven't already.

So what can you expect when you find a practitioner who offers integrative medicine? Don't worry: you won't see any voodoo dolls or kettles brewing strange potions. What you *will* experience is a combination of traditional Western medicine with some appropriate alternative or complementary therapies - think things like massage, yoga, herbal medicine, acupuncture, stress reduction techniques, biofeedback, nutrition counseling, or exercise coaching.

Simply put, your practitioner will thoroughly evaluate *you* - all of you, including your mind, body, and spirit - and will come up with a plan that includes a combination of therapies best suited to restore you to optimum wellness.

It's about time.

Now you know the basics, and you have a good idea of where to start. So get started! Keep reading, and you'll learn even more about how to achieve wellness, starting right now.

Chapter 2

Stress and Resilience: Powerful Examples of the Mind-Body-Spirit Model

How Stressed Are You?

Before you read any more, it might be fun to find out where you stand when it comes to stress! The Stress Management Society has a great online quiz that will help you determine how vulnerable you are to stress.

Access stress test at:

stress.org.uk

Symptoms of Stress

Body
headaches, frequent infections, taut muscles, muscular twitches, fatigue, skin irritations, breathlessness

Mind
worrying, muddled thinking, impaired judgment, nightmares, indecisions, negativity, hasty decisions

Behavior
accident prone, loss of appetite, loss of sex drive, drinking more, insomnia, restlessness, smoking more

Emotions
loss of confidence, more fussy, irritability, depression, apathy, alienation, apprehension

Chapter 2
Stress and Resilience
Powerful Examples of the Mind-Body-Spirit Model

The truth is that stress doesn't come from your boss, your kids, your spouse, traffic jams, health challenges, or other circumstances. It comes from your thoughts about your circumstances.
Andrew Bernstein, author

One of the most essential things you can do to improve your health and boost your longevity is *manage* stress. It's that simple - and that important. And, fortunately, regardless of your circumstances, it's within your power to do exactly that.

Before we talk about how to manage stress, let's start with some basics. We all have stress; it starts the minute we're born (or even before) and doesn't end until we take our last breath. We have to have *some* stress - it's what keeps our body functioning. It's when stress gets chronic or out of control that problems start.

If you're like most other Americans, you're all too familiar with what stress feels like. According to the American Institute of Stress, 90 percent of all American adults experience high levels of stress once or twice a week. Maybe they're the lucky ones: a fourth of all American adults, says the Institute, are burdened by crushing levels of stress *nearly every day*. That's not all: only 29 percent of Americans feel like they're doing a decent job of managing their stress. That's significant, because stress wreaks major damage on your body and can even shorten your life. It's also significant because people under stress tend to cope with it in unhealthy ways - by doing things like eating poorly, failing to exercise, smoking, and picking up other bad habits.

30

And while you may think stress results only from bad stuff, think again.

There are actually two kinds of stress. *Distress* is caused by negative events in your life - you have a classroom of extremely challenging students, your parent dies, you get divorced, you're stuck in a traffic jam on your way to an important conference, your child is diagnosed with a chronic illness. *Eustress*, on the other hand, is caused by things you usually think of as "good" or happy - you get married, you are recognized as teacher of the year, your financial situation improves, you and your partner are finally expecting the baby you've wanted, or it's Christmas.

And, believe it or not, both bad stress and good stress impact your health.

Stress and its health-related disorders pack a powerful punch: The American Academy of Family Physicians estimates that two-thirds of all office visits to family doctors are the result of stress-related symptoms. The American Institute of Stress thinks the percentage is more along the line of 75 percent.

Stress can also shorten your life. Different studies tend to show different percentages, but one thing is certain: chronic, unremitting stress significantly increases your risk of premature death.

About this time, you might be feeling like you need to move into a bubble, but fear not: we're going to help you understand what stress is, how your body responds to it, how to protect yourself from its effects, and how to successfully manage it.

You'll learn, too, a very important fact: stress can be either "good" or "bad" for you, and that all depends on how you deal with it. If your stress is chronic or uncontrolled, it can make you sick. Literally. But if you manage it well, it can be energizing, stimulating, and can result in growth.

What is Stress?

So what, exactly, is *stress*? Simply stated, stress is anything that upsets your body's internal balance, causing it to adapt. That includes physical illness or injury. When something - good or bad - happens to upset that internal balance (called *homeostasis*), your body kicks into gear with a series of reactions; together, they make up what's known as the *stress response*.

Effects Of Stress

- **Hair:** Excessive hair loss & baldness

- **Muscles:** Neck & shoulder pain, musculoskeletal aches, lower back pain

- **Digestive tract:** Diseases of the digestive tract including gastritis, stomach ulcers and irritable colon

- **Skin:** Outbreak of skin problems, such as eczema and psoriasis

- **Brain:** Insomnia, headaches, irritability, anxiety & depression

- **Mouth:** Oral ulcers & excessive dryness

- **Heart:** Cardiovascular disease & hypertension

- **Lungs:** Exacerbate asthmatic conditions

- **Reproductive organs:** Menstrual disorders and recurrent vaginal infections in women & impotence in men

What is Stress?

Stress: the unconscious preparation to fight or flee that a person experiences when faced with any demand

Stressor: the person or event that triggers the stress response

Distress: the adverse psychological, physical, behavioral, and organizational consequences that may arise as a result of stressful events

Strain: distress

There are probably as many specific types of stress as there are victims of stress, but we can pretty much group them into three general categories:

- *Psychological stress* - the type we most often associate with the term *stress* - results from the way you mentally and emotionally react to any kind of threat. Your body responds in the same way whether the threat is real or imagined.
- *Physical stress* results from things in your environment that upset your body's equilibrium. These include things like constant noise, air pollution, bacteria or viruses that cause illness, overcrowding, an inadequate supply of clean drinking water, excessive exertion, or extreme heat or cold. It also results from illness or injury.
- *Social stress* results from conflicts in your interpersonal relationships or with people around you - an argument with your spouse, a misunderstanding with the principal, the challenge of dealing with a perpetually angry student. Social stress can also result from prolonged isolation or the inability to make friends and feel at ease among people.

Regardless of the type of stress, the body's response is the same. The nervous system goes on high alert, a cascade of hormones is released throughout the body, and the immune system is slammed. It's all part of the stress response, an exquisitely designed reaction that served our ancient ancestors brilliantly but that isn't suited very well for folks in our day and age.

Four Stages of the Stress Response

Stage 1	Stage 2	Stage 3	Stage 4
Stimuli from one or more of the five senses are sent to the brain	The brain deciphers the stimulus as either a threat or a non-threat	The body stays activated until the threat is over	The body returns to homeostasis once the threat is gone

Stress Response

You may have heard of the stress response by another name: the *flight-or-fight response*. It came in very handy for early man, who faced a whole different set of dangers than we do. Let's set up a quick scenario to show what it looked like. Imagine that Og, the local caveman, sets out early one morning to hunt for game to feed his family. As he stealthily creeps down a grassy path he's frequented many times, he suddenly hears the breathy panting of a cat - a *big* cat. Og has come face-to-face with a large tiger, who is coincidentally also out hunting for game.

Stress is your (chosen) response to a (perceived) threat. You've got the *power* to *overcome* it!

Fight   **Flight**

At this precise moment, Og experiences stress. He has two choices: he can run (flight) in an attempt to save his life, or he can try to dominate the tiger (fight), also in an attempt to save his life. Before he even has a chance to decide what to do, his body launches a hair-trigger response that will perfectly equip him to do either one.

That's all well and good - for a caveman. It's not so handy for us: running away or fighting aren't exactly the appropriate responses when we face the stress of a recertification exam, a less-than-stellar performance review, stomach flu on the way to Disneyland, harassing calls from a bill collector, the frustrating inability to conceive a child after years of trying, or a flat tire on the interstate. But try telling that to your body, which responds to *your* stresses exactly the way Og's body responded to *his*.

In fact, the dozen reactions involved in the stress response treat every stressor - the flat tire, the broken shoelace, the baby who won't stop crying - like it's a life-threatening event, even though you clearly know it's not. Because, reasons the stress response, what if it really is a tiger ready to pounce on you and make you tonight's main course?

Here they are - the twelve responses that happen with split-second speed and accuracy whenever you experience stress:

1 Your adrenal glands, situated on top of your kidneys, start pumping out stress hormones (cortisol and catecholamines). These hormones are essential for life; you need them *in the right amount*. But when the adrenal glands go crazy and start flooding your system with those hormones, very bad things happen. They can impair your immune system and make it tough for you to fight off disease (even something as simple as the common cold). And the result of too much of these stress hormones can lead to disaster: your lymph glands (part of your immune system) shrivel. Your bones get brittle. Your blood pressure spikes; so does your blood sugar, (sometimes high enough to mimic diabetes). The memory cells in your brain start to shrink.

2 Your thyroid gland then starts pumping out thyroid hormones. That was good for Og: these hormones speed up metabolism so the body's fuel is burned more quickly (preparing for flight or fight). But you're not Og, and here's what happens to you: You get shaky. You have insomnia. You can't tolerate heat. You are exhausted. In fact, this is the reason some people lose weight when under chronic stress . . . but it's not a diet we'd recommend.

3 The hypothalamus in your brain releases endorphins. These powerful natural painkillers enabled Og and his associates to fight or flee even when they were injured. Okay, you're probably thinking, what's so bad about getting a dose of natural painkillers? The way we're programmed today, those endorphins actually *deplete* other important pain-relieving hormones, including serotonin, dopamine, and norepinephrine; you end up with a headache, backache, even arthritis pain. But that's not all. Your hypothalamus also secretes a bad boy called CRH (corticotropin-releasing hormone), which is the key chemical that kicks off the stress response. With CRH circulating through your system, you're on constant alert for danger and far too over-responsive to stimuli of any kind. Simply put, you're always waiting for the other shoe to drop.

4 Your sex hormones - progesterone if you're a woman, testosterone if you're a man - practically dry up and blow away. Again, that served Og and his friends well;

Types of Stress

Nutritional Stress
Vitamin and mineral deficiencies, food intolerances and allergies, sugar overload, artificial sweeteners and flavors, chemical preservatives.

Psychospiritual Stress
Troubled relationships, financial pressure, career dissatisfaction, challenges reaching life goals, spiritual alignment and general state of happiness

Physical and Traumatic Stress
Subluxations of the spine, intense labor, sleep deprivation, injuries, surgical procedures, illness and infection

Chemical Stress
Caffeine, alcohol, nicotine, drugs, pesticides, environmental pollutants and other chemical toxins

Mental/Emotional Stress
Sadness, anger, guilt, fear, shame, worry, anxiety, overwork, perfectionism, and other negative feelings.

people had little interest in each other sexually during times of decreased food supply, drought, or overcrowding, all of which caused stress for them. The same thing happens to you when stress becomes chronic. You suffer from sexual dysfunction (like inability to reach orgasm), lose your sex drive, or become infertile. If you're a woman, chronic stress can mess with your menstrual periods, making them early, irregular, or absent.

5 Your digestive tract shuts down. Here's why: the blood required for digestion was needed to fuel the muscles, giving Og superhuman strength to either run or fight. The same thing happens to you. Eating while you're under stress leads to a laundry list of digestive complaints: nausea, bloating, abdominal discomfort, constipation, and diarrhea, to name just a few. And don't forget dry mouth. In fact, dry mouth is such a reliable symptom of stress that it's used in China as a lie detector test.

6 Glucose (blood sugar) is released into your bloodstream to give you extra fuel; immediately afterward, insulin floods your system so your body can metabolize the extra fuel. Og needed the resulting short-term burst of energy. You *don't* need it. In fact, it can cause abnormally high or low blood sugar, high blood pressure, high cholesterol, weight gain, and increased risk of heart disease.

7 Glucose and insulin gave you short-term energy; now your liver secretes cholesterol into your bloodstream, which gave Og's muscles sustained energy. You don't need any more cholesterol. So your body just deposits the excess in your blood vessels, and voila - another risk factor for cardiovascular disease.

8 Your heart starts racing so it can pump more blood to your muscles and lungs, delivering more fuel and oxygen to the muscles. It prepared Og to flee or fight; all you get is sustained high blood pressure, which can result in cardiovascular and kidney disease.

9 Your lungs work harder and your breathing rate increases; Og needed the increased air supply to meet his threats. Sadly, the increased breathing that happens in response to stress is usually shallow and high in the chest, which actually *decreases* the amount of oxygen available to your system.

10 Your blood gets thick and coagulates more easily. That helped Og in case he got wounded - the wound stopped bleeding more quickly. That's not any kind of benefit to you, though; you can end up with blood clots, heart attack, stroke, or a potentially fatal embolus (a blood clot that breaks away and lodges in your heart, lung, or brain).

11 Your skin blanches, sweats, and seems to "crawl." This reaction cooled off Og's overheated muscles and diverted blood away from his wounds. All it does for you is make you blanche, sweat, and feel like your skin is "crawling."

12 Finally, all five of your senses become sharper. Og used that to his advantage with enhanced night vision, the ability to hear a predator from a distance, and a sharper sense of touch. When under chronic stress, however, your senses are on constant red alert. You feel pain in response to things that shouldn't cause pain - you might get a headache, for example, from exposure to light, sound, or certain smells. And you might get nausea, cramping, and diarrhea when your "gut signals" get amplified.

Put it all together, and the stress response involves a complicated series of more than 1,400 known chemical reactions in your body. At this point you might be wondering why anyone is still left standing. So here's the really important thing to remember about those 1,400 chemical reactions: if you only experience them once in a while, you're okay.

It really is a matter of quantity.

Because when stress becomes chronic, you will begin to suffer the harsh effects described above. And if your stress is unremitting, you will almost certainly pay a horrific price.

The very latest research shows that we have three options for responding to anything our system thinks is a threat. The first is the classic stress response: mobilization (or, in other words, flight or fight). The twelve responses above kick into gear, and your body is ramped up to either run or fight (just like Og).

The second option is immobilization: you freeze. You might faint, lose consciousness, or become so panic-stricken you literally can't move. That kind of response didn't work well for Og, but does work well for reptiles. It's not so good for you, though - it damages you physically and emotionally and takes you a lot longer to recover from the stressful event.

The third option is social engagement - a series of things like making eye contact with someone else, talking in a calm way, listening in a relaxed way, or using touch in an appropriate and calm way. We humans are the only ones who can use this third option, something that immediately begins to calm you, stop the classic flight-or-fight response, and override your body's reaction to something it perceives as a threat.

How the Body Reacts to Stress

Remember what we said earlier about stress: it's anything that requires the body to adapt. Eight decades ago, a scientist named Hans Selye - a pioneer in stress research - figured out that the adaptation occurs in three stages. He called it the *general adaptation syndrome*. It may be eight decades old, but its science is every bit as compelling today as it was back when America was easing its way out of the Great Depression.

Seyle's General Adaption Syndrome

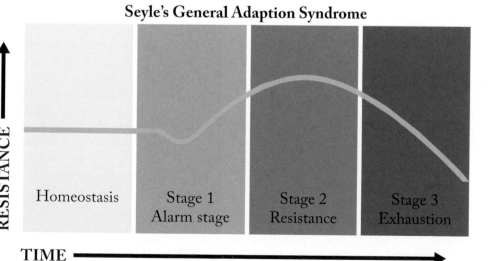

RESISTANCE

Homeostasis | Stage 1 Alarm stage | Stage 2 Resistance | Stage 3 Exhaustion

TIME ➡

Once you understand these three stages, it's easy to see why it's so important to limit the amount of stress you experience. In fact, it makes a lot of sense. Here, then, are the three all-important stages of the general adaptation syndrome:

Alarm Reaction

In this, the first stage, the sirens go off and the body is alerted: incoming stress! With astonishing speed, the body pounds through the twelve reactions of the stress response like so many dominoes going down in sequence. And before you even realize it, your body is pumped up, stoked to the hilt, ready to meet the challenge.

Here's the great part: Every episode of stress eventually ends. And if the stress is relatively brief, your reaction is limited to the first stage - the alarm reaction. That means your body's *reaction* to the stress ends, too. In other words, your body bounces back and everything returns to normal.

You experience a quick adaptive response. You pick yourself up, brush yourself off, and go on with life. The twelve reactions of the stress response are actually ideally suited to this kind of short-term experience.

The kind of stress you experience in this case is called *acute stress*, and it generally lasts anywhere from a few minutes to a few hours (think the stress of giving a presentation at a professional conference or the stress of getting stuck in a traffic jam that will make you significantly late to work). If you are successfully managing your stress, you'll be limited to this kind of stress and this kind of reaction.

Resistance

Now let's look at what happens when stress gets a little more serious. Instead of experiencing short, occasional bouts of stress, you find that your stress is more prolonged - it's more intense, it happens more frequently, or it takes an extended period to resolve. In this case, the stress lasts for several hours or longer, and you may experience stress numerous times in a week. When that happens, your body reacts with resistance.

Here's what happens: Your body's not ready to bail . . . not yet, at least. It actually steps up all its systems so that everything is up to par and poised to meet the challenge. And the system that is boosted the most, interestingly, is the immune system. It's your body's way of trying to position you to resist getting sick so you can stay healthy enough to battle the stress.

Increased immunity sounds great, doesn't it? Yes, but not *this* increased. Your supercharged immune system can cause all kinds of disorders associated with excess immunity - at its simplest, things like allergies; at its most complex, things like rheumatoid arthritis or lupus or other autoimmune diseases (in which the immune system attacks the body's own tissues). Here's the really tricky part: When this happens, the immune system develops a "memory" of how it is responding to the challenge. When the next challenge (stress) comes along, the immune system will rely on its memory, and you might have a very radical response to a rather simple experience.

If the stress eventually resolves, things eventually return to normal, but not without some difficulties along the way. If the stress doesn't resolve, the body moves on to the next reaction.

Exhaustion (Dysregulation)

Simply put, the body has its limits. Those limits are different in every person, but each body has its limits. And when your body reaches its limit, it breaks down. The kind of stress that causes this reaction is chronic stress, or stress that lasts for months or even years.

When this kind of chronic stress doesn't relent, the body eventually loses its ability to keep up with the demands. Among the first to go is the immune function that protects the body against illness and disease and helps it heal from infection. At its least serious, you will have increased susceptibility to infections, such as the common cold, and you'll have a tougher time getting better. At its most serious, infections can become rampant, impacting the entire body.

What about Hassles?

You know all about hassles - those annoying, seemingly minor inconveniences that crop up on an almost daily basis. You get stranded behind a blisteringly slow woman in the checkout line when you've got only minutes to get home. You choose the bathroom stall that's out of toilet paper. You're trying to get an important presentation done on a computer with a slow Internet speed. You run out of gas on the way to work.

Certainly hassles can't fall in the same category as *stress* - or can they?
Believe it or not, research shows that sometimes it's not the major stressful events but the minor hassles that accumulate and eventually cause problems. A number of studies show that illness, which is often associated only with major stressful events, can actually result from hassles even when no stress events have occurred. Most commonly associated with an accumulation of hassles are headaches, stomach distress, chest pain, and backaches.

Sometimes hassles follow a stressful event, and they can make the impact of the stress even worse. Psychiatrist and behavioral scientist Ian Wickramsekera makes the point by using the example of a man whose wife has died. The death of his wife is obviously a major stressor. But then come the hassles as he morphs into the role of father *and* housekeeper: needing to cook the meals, dress the children, do the laundry, help with homework, pay the bills, and all the other things his wife used to do. They become hassles, and they exacerbate the stress of coping with his wife's death.

So don't brush off the effect of hassles. Remember that they, too, need to be managed in the same way you learn to manage stress.

The Specific Effects of Stress

Stress - not the once-in-a-while kind you bounce back from, but the chronic kind that can cause real damage - has been shown to have specific effects on practically all the body systems, literally from head to toe.

Let's start at the top. Here's a real irony: the hormones that are supposed to protect vital brain cells actually *kill* those brain cells when there are too many of them for too long a time. The result? Impaired thinking and reduced memory. When rats were exposed to prolonged stress (five days a week for six months), they showed reduced electrical activity in the central memory area of the brain. In autopsies, they had lost twice as many brain cells (a stunning 50 percent) as their pals who had not been exposed to stress.

> *Sometimes it is not the mountain in front of you but the grain of sand in your shoe that brings you to your knees.*
>
> Ian Wickramsekera

Effects Of Chronic Stress

Brain and Nerves
Headaches, feeling of despair, lack of energy, sadness, nervousness, anger, irritability, trouble concentrating, memory problems, difficulty sleeping, mental health disorders (anxiety, panic attacks, depression, etc.)

Heart
Faster heartbeat or palpitations, rise in blood pressure, increased risk of high cholesterol and heart attack

Stomach
Nausea, stomach ache, heartburn, weight gain, increased or decreased appetite

Pancreas
Increased risk of diabetes

Intestines
Diarrhea, constipation and other digestive problems

Reproductive Organs
For women-irregular or painful periods, reduced sexual desire. For men-impotence, low sperm production, reduced sexual desire

Other
Acne and order skin problems, muscle aches and tension, increased risk for low bone density and weakened immune system (making it harder to fight off or recover from illnesses)

There's more. Prolonged stress can cause brain cells to shrink and can impair the development of new nerve pathways in the brain - something that can happen in as few as three weeks of unremitting stress. And here's one that speaks to a universal concern: studies show that stress can play a role in the development and progression of Alzheimer's disease.

Moving along to the heart and the cardiovascular system, stress is a major contributor to cardiovascular disease. Stress causes high blood pressure, which damages the lining of the blood vessels; in an attempt to repair the damage, the body deposits fats in the arteries and clots start to form. Stress also causes the heart to beat faster, elevates cholesterol levels, causes the narrowing of blood vessels, and leads to heart attack and stroke.

Now let's look at the gastrointestinal system. All kinds of stomach and bowel disorders have been linked to stress, especially irritable bowel syndrome. And here's an interesting finding: the effect of stress on the digestive system seems to depend on the *perception* of stress. A thirteen-year study found that people who perceived they were under stress were more likely to develop stomach ulcers than those who perceived they were not stressed, regardless of reality.

Finally, the link between stress and impaired immunity is powerful. The very hormones that are released during the stress response cripple the immune system. But there's good news: you can moderate that effect dramatically through physical resilience (things like eating well, getting enough sleep, and staying active) and through factors like optimism, a sense of control, strong social support, and good coping mechanisms.

Perception Is the Name of the Game

You've probably noticed that *perception* has been peppered throughout this discussion of stress - and there's a very good reason for that. Just as each individual has his or her own limits, each individual copes with and responds to stress differently. The way in which you think and how you perceive stress has a significant impact on how well you are able to manage stress and resist its effects.

Researchers have discovered that a number of things influence the way you cope with stress. There is some evidence that there may be a genetic factor involved; fascinating research in New Zealand indicates that some people may be born with a genetic tendency to either be more vulnerable to stress or to be more resilient to stress.

The ability to cope with stress may also be related to your coping ability in general. And that, too, may be something with which you were born. But the most important factor in coping with stress and its effects appears to be

*It's not the **stress** that kill us, it is our reaction to it.*

Hans Selye

perception. In fact, your *perception* about the stress event is more important than the event itself. That's pretty powerful stuff.

To show how crucial perception is, one researcher came up with a great example of how quickly perception can change the impact of a stressful experience:

Imagine you and a friend are hiking in the woods; you're out in front and enjoying the experience immensely. Suddenly, as you round a bend in the trail, you see a rattlesnake coiled up in the dust immediately in front of you, poised to strike. Talk about the flight-or-fight syndrome! Your entire body tenses and you prepare to run for your life.

Just then your companion catches up with you and, seeing the snake, starts to laugh. "Look at that rubber rattlesnake some kid left on the trail!" he says. Suddenly you go from feeling the most intense stress you can remember to - what? Embarrassment? ("I can't believe I fell for that.") Anger? ("How dare someone do something that thoughtless!")

Hang on a minute. The situation is *exactly the same*. You're on the same hiking trail in the woods you were on just seconds ago, staring at the same coiled snake that caught your attention just seconds ago. But your perception has changed, and so has everything else. The snake itself didn't cause any of your feelings - not the stress, the embarrassment, or the anger. The way you *thought about* the snake is what caused your feelings.

Your own thoughts, your own perception, created the meaning that led to everything you felt. And that's how stress works.

Perception is also a key to managing stress. We'll talk more about that later. For now, let's say you're on a canoe in a swiftly flowing stream, catapulting at a high rate of speed as your boat is carried by the currents. You can either grip the oars, clench your jaw, and hang on for dear life as you liken yourself to a passenger on a runaway train - or you can throw your head back, laugh at the top of your lungs, and enjoy the ride.

It's all up to you.

When it comes to stress, the body is responding to what's going on in the brain, not to what's going on in the environment.

Margaret Kemeny, Director, Health Psychology and Behavioral Neuroscience Program, UCSF

The greatest weapon against stress is our ability to choose one thought over another.

William James

Life is based on perception. Perception is based on opinion. Opinion is based of thought. Thought comes from the mind. Change your mind, change your life.

Resilience

Another crucial factor is *resilience*, the ability to withstand stress and catastrophe and to adapt to life's setbacks. People who are resilient suffer the same kinds of hassles, stresses, and painful events we all do - but they have figured out how to harness an inner strength that enables them to adapt, no matter the circumstances. Resilient people have an amazing ability to rebuild, even after devastating tragedy. When they are hurt, they figure out a way to make everything turn out well. Simply put, they learn valuable lessons from life's bumps and bruises.

How Resilient Are You?

Wondering how resilient you are? Take the online quiz developed by The Resiliency Center. Access it at: *resiliencyquiz.com*

People who are resilient avoid the trap of seeing a crisis as an insurmountable problem that will leave them destroyed. They realize that change is an unavoidable part of living, and they take decisive action to resume working toward their goals. They refuse to let a stress or failure in one area spill over into other parts of their lives. They don't dwell on failures or blame themselves for what went wrong; instead, they learn from their mistakes and move forward. They stay flexible. They see stresses or setbacks as challenges to be overcome, and they move ahead with a sense of commitment and control. Above all, they keep things in perspective - both the stresses or failures *and* the potential solutions.

I haven't failed. I've simply found 10,000 ways that won't work.

Thomas Edison

American inventor Thomas Edison is a great example of someone with resilience. You know him as the guy who invented the incandescent light bulb - but did you know that he built literally thousands of prototypes of his light bulb before he finally got it right? He simply refused to give up, and he bounced back from every failure. And his incredible resilience gave us not only the light bulb, but motion pictures, the phonograph, and the telegraph.

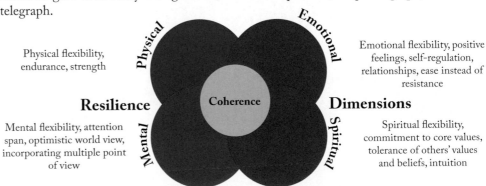

Physical flexibility, endurance, strength

Physical

Emotional

Emotional flexibility, positive feelings, self-regulation, relationships, ease instead of resistance

Resilience

Coherence

Dimensions

Mental flexibility, attention span, optimistic world view, incorporating multiple point of view

Mental

Spiritual

Spiritual flexibility, commitment to core values, tolerance of others' values and beliefs, intuition

People who aren't resilient experience the opposite. When they are exposed to stress, upset, hurt, or distress, they start feeling helpless, dwell on their problems, feel overwhelmed, and see themselves as victims instead of someone who can grow through the experience. The resilient people are able to avoid the problems associated with stress. The people who aren't resilient are the ones who fall victim to stress and its devastating effects.

So how do people become resilient? They grow through difficulty, figure out better ways of thinking (perception), and develop management skills that help them to not only become more resilient but to better cope with stress. A variety of thoughts, behaviors, and actions contribute to resilience, and they can be learned and developed throughout life.

Researchers have found that certain traits contribute to resiliency:
- Self-confidence and a belief in your strengths and capabilities
- A sense of general control
- Finding meaning in your life and the things you do
- The ability to see yourself as resilient instead of seeing yourself as a victim
- Close, supportive relationships with parents, family members, and friends
- A willingness to reach out to others for help in times of trouble
- Cultural traditions or beliefs that value coping skills
- Good communication and problem-solving skills
- The flexibility to adapt to new or different situations and challenges
- The ability to manage strong impulses and emotions
- The desire to help others
- Coping with stress in healthy ways

How to Manage Stress and Develop Resiliency

Whole books have been written on how to manage stress. That should tell you one important thing: there are almost countless ways to help you get on top of things when you find yourself overloaded - stressed to a point that you've tumbled outside your comfort zone.

How do you know you're outside your comfort zone? The scary thing is that the effects of stress can creep up on you. One minute you think you're fine, and the next minute you're dealing with a cascade of signs and symptoms that let you know you're *not* fine at all.

One of the first keys to managing stress is to know when enough is enough. If you monitor yourself carefully and watch for the following signs, you can more likely get on top of stress before it gets out of hand:

Physical symptoms. Watch for the following things you can't attribute to any other cause: aches and pains, chest pain, rapid heartbeat, nausea, diarrhea or constipation, dizziness, loss of sex drive, or frequent colds or other infections.

Mental or cognitive symptoms. You're likely experiencing an unhealthy overload of stress if you experience anxiety, racing thoughts, constant worry, poor judgment, an inability to concentrate, or memory problems.

Emotional symptoms. Irritability, depression, general unhappiness, moodiness, agitation, an inability to relax, a hair-trigger temper, or a sense of isolation or loneliness are emotional responses that can occur when stress has driven you out of your comfort zone.

Behavioral symptoms. You are likely overloaded with stress if you are procrastinating or neglecting things for which you're responsible, are isolating yourself from others, or have developed new nervous habits (like pacing or biting your nails). Watch, too, for changes in your behavior - sleeping too much or too little, eating too much or too little, or starting to use tobacco, alcohol, or drugs to relax.

If you recognize yourself in any of those descriptions, it's time to take action - you need to try some of the following approaches to manage your stress.

- This sounds pretty basic, and it is, but it's also key to the whole stress-management process: figure out what is causing your stress. You *might* be stressed by a number of things at once, but you're more likely to be facing just one or two big stressors. The rest are just tagging along, hassling you and adding to your grief. Pinpoint what is causing you the most stress so you can make a plan, get organized, and take decisive action.

- Keep a stress journal. Write down what you think and how you feel about the things that are stressing you out. Rate the intensity of your feelings. Record what does and doesn't work in your effort to manage or get rid of the stressor. Over time, you'll likely be able to identify the triggers that cause you stress.

- Determine what you can control and what you can't. Change your way of thinking about the things you can't control (the high unemployment rate in your area) and focus on doing something about the things you can control (the number of job applications you fill out and the ways you can improve your resume).

- Remember the importance of how you perceive things. Work on ways to improve.

- Simplify. You can't do it all—no one can.

- Get others to share the load. That works equally well at work as at home. Other teachers might be able to pitch in together and lighten things for everyone, or maybe your school could benefit from volunteers or interns. Create a plan and take it to the office—you might be surprised with what can be done!

- Control who and what surrounds you. If a particular friend is wearing you out, find a tactful and courteous way to scale way back on the amount of time you spend together.

- Value and build the friendships that are good for you. Talking over your issues with a trusted friend can not only be a source of comfort, but can help you sort out and identify issues you've been unclear about.

- Participate in social activities and engagements that you value and enjoy. Building a strong social network is an important way of coping with stress.

- Establish boundaries and stick to them.

- While you're at it, manage your time well and then protect that time. Decide what you're willing to do, then be very cautious about taking on any more. Start by getting more organized—go through that enormous pile of stuff and get it filed away in order.

- Stop procrastinating.

- Schedule time for leisure and/or personal time every single day. Put it on the calendar and honor it just as you would an important meeting. The time you spend isn't as important as how you spend it. It might seem impossible at first, but you'll find it might be the most important thing you do all day.

- Turn off your phone and step away from the computer for part of every day.

- Take a hot bath or shower when you're feeling uptight. If you can, relax in a hot tub.

- Do something you love every single day. If your job is causing an overload of stress right now, find a hobby you love and spend time on it every day, even if it's just fifteen minutes or half an hour. Think about what brought you the greatest joy when you were growing up, and go back to those activities. That's easier than you think—there are even plenty of challenging and fun coloring books for adults on the market!

- Try relaxation techniques, such as mindfulness techniques, meditation, deep breathing techniques, or yoga. If you don't know how to get started, there are online tutorials as well as classes offered by gyms, community colleges, and other programs in most areas.

- Take care of yourself, even if there seem to be a tsunami of other demands threatening to pummel you. Eat healthy food, get enough exercise, and get plenty of sleep; most experts recommend eight hours a night.

- Prepare for the next day the night before, and get up fifteen minutes earlier in the morning. Allow fifteen minutes of extra time to get to work and to get to any appointments during the day.

- Get rid of the stuff that doesn't *really* have to be done. Have you volunteered for too many things? Does your entire faculty really need to meet every week? Could you arrange a carpool to get your kids to their activities some of the time? Pick away at your to-do list and make sure everything on it is supporting your goals and values and is giving your life meaning. Learn to say no.

- Don't be afraid to make mistakes. There's something to learn from each one (remember Thomas Edison?). The self-imposed need to be perfect is in itself a major stressor.

- Create a variety of stress-management techniques to help you in different types of situations. The one-size-fits-all mantra doesn't work here any better than it works in the fitting room.

Don't try to do every single thing on this list - that alone could cause stress! Instead, read through the list and think carefully about every suggestion. Depending on what's causing your stress, you will likely find that a handful of suggestions can go a long way toward helping you manage the stress and cope better with the unique challenges you're facing.

What about developing resilience? Many of the same suggestions work toward helping you learn resilience. In addition to any techniques you decide to try for stress management, try some of the following approaches for developing resilience:

Ways to Develop Resiliency

- Make sure you're managing your stress.

- Take care of yourself.

- Build strong relationships in your family and among your friends; seek out people who will support you and believe in you.

- Engage in things that are exciting and stimulating, and use your successes to build self-confidence.

- Set goals, even small ones, that will help you accomplish things on a regular basis.

- Do something meaningful every day.

- Whenever something difficult happens, immediately look for the solution. Value the chance to learn from whatever comes your way. Don't ignore it, because it won't go away. Learn from your mistakes - keep looking until you identify a lesson that will help you in the future.

- Maintain perspective; things may be tough right now, but they will get better.

- Stay positive. Look for the silver lining in every cloud, because it's there. And remember that no one can be positive all the time; the important thing is that you're positive more often than you're negative.

- If you have a good sense of humor, hang on to it and use it, especially if the going gets tough. If you don't have a lot of humor in your life, do more things that make you laugh - because laughter is powerful medicine. Go see a funny movie, catch a local comic at an improv theater, or read a hilarious book.

- Make it a practice to notice the positive things in every experience.

- Treat people with compassion and empathy.

- Remember that you can choose your response. You can get upset or you can move on.

- Be proactive. Come up with a strong plan to confront any problems, and then execute your plan with determination.

- Stay hopeful.

Developing Resilience

1) Create a personal vision

2) Feel in control

3) Be flexible

4) Get organzied

5) Be able to solve problems

6) Get connected

7) Be socially competent

8) Be proactive

Recipe for Resilience

7 1/2 hours of sleep

10 minutes of meditation or prayer

25 minutes intense exercise

2 acts of generosity

1 hug from family or friend

3 dollops joy

Combine evenly and enjoy frequently. Make daily for long-term benefits.

Chapter 3

Perception and Personality: Their Impact on Health and Wellness

Chapter 3
Perception and Personality:
Their Impact on Health and Wellness

What you see and what you hear depends a great deal on where you are standing. It also depends on what sort of person you are.
C.S. Lewis

Scholar, philosopher, and emperor Marcus Aurelius made an astute observation in the second century A.D. that modern medicine has proved to be remarkably accurate almost two thousand years later: "Reject your sense of injury, and the injury itself disappears." In other words, much of how *you see things* determines how things are in your life.

And based on the findings of a significant amount of research, we can take things a step farther: how you see the world (your perceptions), how you interpret what you see (your explanatory style), and even your personality can go a long way toward determining whether you will stay healthy and live long. As the brilliant composer Irvin Berlin put it, "Life is 10 percent what you make it and 90 percent how you take it."

All kinds of people - starting with Marcus Aurelius - have weighed in on the importance of perception and personality for several thousand years, and they're right. If this is the first you've heard of it, start right now to recognize that the way you see things is critical to how well you are. And understand one very important thing: It's within your power to change. So wherever you find yourself right now, you can start today to make the changes that will improve your health, your well-being, and your longevity.

In this chapter we'll let you in on what has been discovered about the way you see things, how you explain what happens, how much control you feel over your life, and even certain aspects of your personality. And then we'll give some helpful tips on how to make even small changes that can improve your odds of staying well.

"All things are subject to interpretation. Whichever interpretation prevails at a given time is a function of power and not truth."

Friedrich Nietzsche

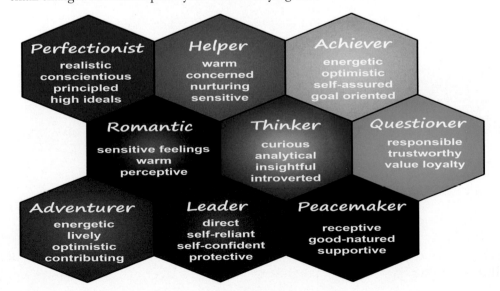

How Do You Explain Things?

We talked a lot about perception in Chapter 2, especially how perception affects stress management. In this chapter, we're going to introduce an important term that goes hand-in-hand with perception: *explanatory style* is the way you see (perceive) or explain the things that happen in your life. It's not a once-in-a-while deal - it's a *habit*. It's the way you talk to others about the events in your life. Even more important, it's the way you talk to *yourself* about the things that happen in your life.

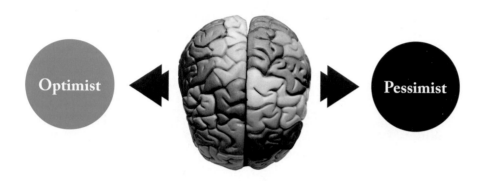

Oh, you're probably thinking, *like optimism and pessimism*. Well, not exactly. Optimism and pessimism are broad personality traits. And they can certainly affect explanatory style (we'll clarify that in a minute). But explanatory style is bigger and more complex than simple optimism and pessimism. It's not only the way you *explain* or see *things*, but it governs the way you *respond to things*. And that's not limited to today - your explanatory style also forms your view of the future and determines how you will behave and react to everything that comes along.

Your explanatory style has three important dimensions:

- It determines whether you see a particular event as fairly isolated or whether you think similar things will keep happening.
- It determines whether you think you have influence or control over what happens to you.
- It determines whether you think a repeated event will always turn out the same or whether the outcome can be changed.

And all three of those things have a significant impact on your health.

Now for the explanation of how optimism and pessimism come in. You have an optimistic explanatory style if you see a particular negative event as not necessarily your fault, something specific only to those particular circumstances, and something that can be changed. That's good news.

If, on the other hand, you see every problem as your fault, believe that everything negative is part of an overall circumstance that will continue to happen forever, and that nothing can change the circumstance or outcome, you have a pessimistic explanatory style. That's not such good news.

> A person's explanatory style is the way they explain events to themselves. This is particularly crucial in the way they interpret their own successes or setbacks. Their conclusions influence whether they become optimistic or pessimistic.

> *We are all in the gutter, but some of us are looking at the stars.*
>
> Oscar Wilde

Imagine that you have a very difficult class this year, complete with a handful of students you know will require a lot of extra time and attention. Let's throw in a couple of kids you know will be discipline problems as well. If you've got an optimistic explanatory style, your thought process will go something like this: *This class is a real challenge, but I'm sure I'll figure out some effective ways to deal with the problems. I've been able to meet similar challenges in the past, and I can do it again.*

▸ **Permanence** ▸ **Pervasiveness** ▸ **Personalization**

	Bad Events	**Good Events**
Optimistic Explanatory Style	Bad events are temporary Bad events are specific Blame other people/circumstances for bad events	Good events are permanent Good events are universal Credit themselves for good events
Pessimistic Explanatory Style	Bad events persist Bad events are universal Blame ourselves for bad events	Good events are temporary Good events are specific Credit other people/circumstances for good events

If you've got a pessimistic explanatory style, your reaction will be quite different: *There's no way I can handle this. I never come out on top in things like this. Why bother? I can't do anything well.*

Where Does It Come From?

So where does explanatory style come from? Are you born with it?

Well, maybe - and maybe not.

Some researchers - including those at the National Institutes of Health and the National Science Foundation - have found a gene at a specific location on the DNA strand that may *influence* an optimistic or pessimistic explanatory style. But scientists at UCLA involved in the same research are quick to point out that this gene is only *one* of the factors that influence explanatory style and that many other factors are likely involved.

A lot of research points to the likelihood that explanatory style is learned, not inherited. These studies indicate that explanatory style comes from three main sources:

- The mother. A mother who consistently delivers positive messages to a child helps that child believe in herself and develop an optimistic outlook.
- Other adults who care for, teach, and/or discipline a child. If these consistently blame a child's character or personality whenever something bad happens, the child will eventually come to believe that he is at fault and things will always go wrong.
- Tragic life events. When something tragic happens in the life of a child - the death of a parent or sibling, the divorce of parents, abuse, or extreme poverty, for example - the child will notice how quickly things are resolved. A child who sees that the results of adversity are temporary will be much more likely to develop an optimistic explanatory style.

Impact on Health?

Your explanatory style is important for a number of reasons, but perhaps the greatest is the fact that it influences your physical and mental health. Here's an interesting fact: our belief about our health - people who *believe* they are in good health and they are able to prevent health problems - is a more powerful predictor of health than a physician using laboratory tests. We all know that cigarette smoking is detrimental to health; studies have shown that smokers are more than twice as likely to die during a twelve-year period than people who don't smoke. Think that's impressive? Well, listen to this: people who believe they're in "poor health" are *seven times* more likely to die in the same period than people who believe they're in "excellent" health - even if their belief is inaccurate.

Researchers think there are a number of factors why. A pessimistic explanatory style frequently leads to depression, and we know that depression hurts the immune system in some really important ways. People who are depressed are also more likely to develop poor health habits - poor diet, lack of exercise, alcohol use, cigarette smoking, failure to wear seatbelts, and so on.

But researchers can't argue with the results on the opposite side of the scale: long-term research shows that an optimistic explanatory style stimulates the immune system, sends positive signals to the body, and engages the body's own healing systems. In numerous studies, those with optimistic explanatory styles enjoy better health, recover more quickly from illness, are less bothered by symptoms they do develop, and live longer.

There's a fascinating reason why things work that way - sophisticated research has shown that the hypothalamic center of the brain, the part that's involved in outlook and attitude, is *directly wired to the immune system*. In other words, positive emotions and attitudes stimulate the immune system and make your body significantly better able to resist and fight diseases and infections of all kind.

And that's just the body. Extensive research also shows that people with an optimistic explanatory style have a significantly better sense of mental well-being and are much less prone to mental disorders, especially anxiety and mood disorders. At least part of that is due to the fact that an optimistic explanatory style improves cognitive responses, increases problem-solving ability, improves coping abilities, and increases the ability to manage stress.

Are You Stuck with It?

So here's the million-dollar question: Once you have a certain explanatory style, are you stuck with it forever? Or can you change?

Change the way you look at things, and the things you look at change.

Wayne W. Dyer

One of the leading pioneers in psychoneuroimmunology emphasizes that explanatory style is really a belief system - and like every other belief system, *it can be changed*. He and other researchers advocate using cognitive therapy as an effective way to change explanatory style. Included in that are developing the ability to recognize how you respond to adversity, identifying how you explain failures to yourself, arguing against your negative responses, and creating new and more accurate beliefs to explain adversity.

If you're hoping to change your explanatory style, consider enlisting the help of a therapist or practitioner who is trained in cognitive therapy. Making the change will require thoughtful, consistent, deliberate practice, but the changes in your style and the improvements in your health make such practice a wise investment.

Are You in Control?

Your explanatory style is only one of the ways you look at things that has a dramatic impact on your health. The other is your sense of control, often called your *locus of control*.

Okay, *locus of control* is a bit of a strange term with which you may not be familiar. Let's start with locus: it's Latin for "place" or "location," and here it means where you think control originates. *An internal locus of control* - the good kind - is your belief that what you do will be effective enough to control your environment. When it comes to health, it's your belief that your health is determined in large part by your behavior. You can see right away why that's a good thing: if you believe you call the shots, you always have the option to change. The National Cancer Institute estimates that nearly half of all cancers might be avoided if people simply avoided risky behavior and got early detection tests - things that only happen if you believe you have the power to affect the outcome.

If the theme song of the external is 'Cast Your Fate to the Winds,' the theme song of the internal is 'I Did It My Way.'

Phillip Rice

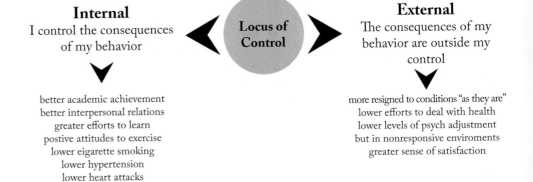

Internal
I control the consequences
of my behavior

Locus of Control

External
The consequences of my
behavior are outside my
control

better academic achievement
better interpersonal relations
greater efforts to learn
postive attitudes to exercise
lower eigarette smoking
lower hypertension
lower heart attacks

more resigned to conditions "as they are"
lower efforts to deal with health
lower levels of psych adjustment
but in nonresponsive enviroments
greater sense of satisfaction

On the other hand, an *external locus of control* is your belief that when it comes to health, you are primarily the victim of external circumstances - things you *can't* change. And when you go through life believing that there's nothing you can do to impact your health, you don't make any behavioral changes, and it all becomes a self-fulfilling prophecy.

To help you understand the concept, let's use an example that's not related to health (because the concept has relevance in all aspects of life). Imagine an "internal" college student who believes she can get good grades if she studies hard, applies herself, refuses to get distracted by friends who are always out partying, and refuses to give up, even when the classes are hard and out of her comfort zone. Guess what? That's exactly what happens. She studies hard, applies herself, stays engaged, and refuses to give up - and she gets good grades.

Now let's look at the "external" college student. He believes he will get bad grades because the teaching assistants design bad tests, the professors grade impulsively and unfairly, and he always has a string of bad luck. So guess what happens to this guy? You're right - he figures that it won't matter if he studies hard, applies himself, stays engaged, or refuses to give up, because according to his very established belief system, nothing he can do matters. So he doesn't do any of those things. And, sure enough, he gets bad grades - another remarkably accurate self-fulfilling prophecy.

Your locus of control isn't a completely black-and-white proposition. You can have an internal locus of control in a lot of areas of your life but an external locus of control in a handful of others. Researchers agree that most people fall somewhere along a continuum between the coveted internal and the dreaded external.

If you're not sure where you stand, there are characteristics that help determine whether you're internal or external. Internals tend to set long-term goals, work hard for achievements, prefer games based on skill, get strong benefits from social supports, tolerate a delay in rewards, are better able to resist coercion, are more willing to take risks, and are much more likely to embark on self-improvement programs. They are less likely to feel depressed, anxious, or helpless, and when they do experience failure, they evaluate what happened and refuse to let that experience predict future failure.

Externals, in contrast, are more likely to lower their goals if things seem too difficult, set short-term goals but avoid thinking about long-term goals, have a difficult time with delayed rewards, prefer games based on chance or luck, are less willing to take risks, are fairly easily coerced by others, and are far less likely to undertake any self-improvement programs. They are more likely to feel helpless or depressed, and when they experience failure they sit around waiting for the other shoe to fall - because of *course* it will happen again.

Where Does It Come From?

Researchers agree that there are a variety of sources that determine your locus of control. One is what kind of parents you had; those who are strict, overly critical, and demand conformity are more likely to produce children who have an external locus of control than do parents who are encouraging, accepting, nurturing, and provide consistent but reasonable discipline. Your childhood socioeconomic status can also play a role - those with lower socioeconomic status may result in parents who feel a low level of control and a high level of insecurity, which can influence the personality development of a child.

Another influence is your larger social environment and cultural factors. Gradual changes in locus of control can reflect changes in culture and society. For example, you might gravitate toward a more internal locus of control if you participate in a society that values individualism, does not tolerate prejudice, and provides greater control over environmental factors, such as technology and birth control. On the other hand, you might gravitate toward a more external locus of control if you live in a society characterized by alienation, cynicism, distrust, a tendency to blame problems on outside forces, and a general "victim" mentality (which can result from a high crime rate or high unemployment rates, for example).

Interestingly, news coverage can also play a role. Researchers have noted that forty years ago, negative, "victimizing" events - such as war, murder, child abduction, natural disasters,

We don't see things as they are, we see them as we are.

Anaïs Nin

and stock market instability - received only brief news coverage. Today, those kinds of things are eagerly broadcast twenty-four hours a day, potentially creating the notion that we're all victims of things we can't control. (We might argue that while it's good to be informed, we *can* control the amount of time we spend watching such coverage - and that staying glued for days at a time to coverage of planes slamming into the Twin Towers might not be the smartest idea.) Partly because of this kind of news coverage, researchers have found that today's young people have a greater external sense of control than did those of forty years ago.

Your prior health experiences can also help determine your locus of control. If you had frequent illnesses during your childhood or adolescence and had slow or difficult recoveries, you are more likely to develop an attitude that external forces are what control or dictate your health.

Finally, your locus of control is influenced tremendously by your general expectations, which are based on your experiences with the world. It's really a cause-and-effect situation: if you pretty consistently realize reward and success from your hard work, you are likely to develop an internal sense of control. If the opposite is true, and you pretty consistently fail regardless of how hard you try, you are likely to develop an external sense of control.

How Does it Impact Health?

Let's start with the obvious: people with an internal locus of control - who believe that their health is a direct result of their own behaviors - have better health. That's partly because they adopt the behaviors (eating a healthy diet, getting regular exercise, practicing effective stress management, avoiding tobacco, using alcohol only in moderation) that protect and improve health. Simple as that.

One of the main reasons a sense of control has a profound impact on health is that people with a good sense of control have healthier immune systems; those who feel helpless or out of control suffer compromised immunity. Another important reason is that your level of control impacts biochemical changes in your brain and the release of important hormones. Internals have much healthier levels of three important hormones: dopamine, which provides a sense of pleasure and reward; norepinephrine, which protects against depression; and serotonin, which relieves pain, regulates mood, and helps control the release of powerful pain-killing brain chemicals, including endorphins.

Above and beyond all that, numerous studies have shown that internals have less risk of illness; externals are more likely to suffer from chronic illness. When illness does strike, internals are more likely to suffer less from symptoms, report less pain, and recover more quickly; externals are just the opposite. Even something as difficult as cancer or AIDS responds in some fairly dramatic ways to locus of control. In a study of long-term AIDS survivors, researchers found that they had a number of characteristics in common, chief among them the fact that they felt a sense of control over their situation. They were the ones who nurtured themselves, took personal responsibility for their disease without considering it a death sentence, felt they were able to influence the outcome of the disease, took control by altering their lifestyles, were assertive, nurtured others with the disease, and were able to effectively communicate their needs. The researchers also found that many of these long-term survivors had previously survived a life-threatening disease, which gave them a much stronger internal locus of control.

You already know that stress can cause illness and even shorten life. Now check out this fact: people with an internal locus of control - those who believe they have at least some control over the stressful situation - suffer *far less* of the physiological damage normally caused by stress. And here's the really cool part: an internal sense of control acts as a "buffer" against stress and its damaging effects if you simply *believe* you have control - even if you really don't.

You Can Change Your Locus of Control

Research supports the fact that you can change your locus of control even if you've had a pretty consistent external locus. To become more internal:

- Start with some specific situations. When you know something is coming up, do everything you can to be completely prepared for the situation. When you're prepared to the best of your ability, you'll feel a much better sense of control. And when that happens over and over, you develop an important new habit.
- Get as much information as you can about any situation you're facing; when you are informed, you are likely to feel much more prepared and able to have control over what happens.
- Identify what or in whom you have a deep level of trust, and learn to rely on that person or thing (a good example is religious faith).
- Work on building a strong support system; include family members, friends, colleagues, and others you can trust.
- Focus on developing a more optimistic outlook. You may need to seek professional help in changing your basic outlook.
- Finally, consider working with a professional to learn new coping skills. There are also a number of good resources and books you can consult to master the skills you need to cope with stressful situations.

Personality: Could Yours Be Making You Sick?

A great deal of research over the last three decades has found that a number of factors - such as, but not limited to, the ones we've already discussed - have a major impact on health and longevity. And here's the exciting thing about that: even if you *do* inherit the tendency for a particular disease, such as heart disease, there are many things you can do to reduce your risk of actually *developing* that disease.

> *You have brains in your head and feet in your shoes, you can steer yourself in any direction you choose!*
>
> Dr Seuss

> *I am not what happened to me, I am what I choose to become.*
>
> Carl Jung

Personality and Health

Lower mortality correlates with high conscientiousness, low neuroticism, high extraversion, and high openness.

There are some very convincing studies that indicate that people may have either a disease-resistant personality or a disease-prone personality - and that, as the names suggest, your personality might either set you up for success or failure when it comes to health and longevity.

What *is* personality, anyway? *Personality* is the set of emotional tendencies, behavioral habits, and personal characteristics that are uniquely you - that set you apart from everyone else. Your personality is what makes you react consistently to situations and stresses in your life and what determines your lifestyle choices. While personality comes partially from what you inherit, it is also powerfully shaped by your environment, the culture that surrounds you, and the family in which you grew up.

Studies conducted over a forty-year period show what researchers call "strong links" between personality and health, but not all agree on exactly how powerful those links are. In fact, there is some controversy and much debate about the impact of personality on health or the connection between specific personality traits and particular diseases. But while the research on personality and health continues and the jury is still out, some findings suggest that certain personality types increase the risk of becoming sick - and much of that has to do with the way certain personalities perceive their health.

Best known among the "disease-prone" personalities is clearly the "type A" personality, which has been strongly linked to heart disease. The type A personality - generally characterized as ambitious, driven, energetic, and impatient - was first linked with a higher risk of heart disease more than fifty years ago, and for decades it was known as the "hurry sickness." More recent research found that the risk of heart disease isn't necessarily higher with type A unless you also have what's called the "toxic core" of the type A personality: anger, suspiciousness, cynicism, excessive self-involvement, and free-floating hostility (a permanent, deep-seated anger that hovers near the surface and explodes with little provocation). We'll talk more about those traits in the next chapter.

Several other "personalities" have been linked to disease. While there has been disagreement among experts, personality types have been linked to cancer, ulcers, asthma, and rheumatoid arthritis. Interestingly, a common factor among all the "disease-prone" personalities is stress, leaving us to wonder whether stress - and not personality - plays the biggest role.

While the disease-prone personality is a matter of some controversy, experts agree on the notion of a "disease-resistant" personality, common traits shared by those who manage to remain well throughout life. Researchers have long known that certain groups of people enjoy remarkably good health and longevity; among them are Mormons, nuns, women who are listed in *Who's Who*, and symphony conductors. We can likely thank a group of personality traits these healthy, long-lived people share: feeling hope, finding meaning in life, enjoying a sense of fulfillment in accomplishments, and finding love.

The Three C's of Hardiness

Control	Commitment	Challenge
Strong sense of control over events in their life, can overcome their experiences	Highly committed and involved in tasks, strong sense of purpose	View life events as challenges to overcome - change is an opportunity for development

Additionally, research indicates that five traits are especially pronounced in people who seem to be able to resist illness. These traits are clustered into a personality known as *hardy* - they have a set of beliefs about themselves and the way in which they interact with the world that enables them to cope with or resist stress. It has been suggested that hardy people develop half as many illnesses as those who are more vulnerable. Hardiness is characterized by:

- An internal sense of control - the belief that you can work to control the outcome of various situations and the willingness to accept responsibility for your choices.
- A sense of challenge, or the ability to see change as an opportunity for creativity, excitement, or growth instead of as a threat. Without a sense of challenge, you are likely to react to change with helplessness, fear, and alienation.
- A sense of commitment in which you believe in the meaningfulness and importance of your experiences and activities and in which you have a healthy sense of curiosity and a commitment to an ideal greater than yourself.
- A feeling of connectedness through which you develop a strong network of social support and through which you feel connected to and relate well with others.
- A feeling of coherence, marked by your belief that things will turn out well and that your environment - internal and external - is fairly predictable.

Researchers may still disagree about the role various personality "types" play in disease, but one thing is clear: you can do a number of things to increase your hardiness and stress resilience, things researchers *do* agree on as ways to protect your health and longevity.

- Become aware of your innermost thoughts and feelings as well as your needs. You might find that you need to be able to get to work early and spend ten to fifteen minutes in your classroom with the door closed to get ready for your day; ask colleagues and administrators to respect your quiet time.
- Identify one or two people in your life who seem to be able to cope well with stressful problems. Then when you find yourself confronted with a challenging situation, imagine how that person would respond - or, better yet, seek advice from him or her on some options you might explore.
- Whenever you experience stress, break your challenges down into small "chunks" that you can more easily confront, then go to work on the easiest ones first.
- Cultivate a fighting spirit that will encourage you to meet challenges head-on.
- Acknowledge difficult emotions and learn to express them appropriately. Then, instead of harboring anger or resentment, move on.
- Change your perspective on problems; try to find the exciting challenges that might result. Taking a recertification exam is stressful, for example, but you can look at it as an opportunity to boost your knowledge, hone your skills, and make yourself more of an asset in the job market.
- If you need to, improve your social network. The key here isn't in the number of family and friends you have, but the *quality*; you need at least a few close and trusted people in whom you can confide.
- Find ways to develop your creativity - learn to play a musical instrument, paint, dance, write, or do something else that will give you a new way of looking at things.
- If you are feeling hopeless about a situation, start by getting as much information as you can about the situation and your options; once you realize you have viable options, work out a game plan to restore a sense of control.
- Every time you see yourself in the mirror, smile at yourself.

Increasing Hardiness and Stress Resilience

Slow down

KEEP CALM

BE positive

TAKE it easy

Unplug!

Enjoy my life

HAVE FUN!

Breathe

RELAX

GO outside

meditate

Chapter 4

The Powerful Effect of Emotions on Health

Chapter 4
The Powerful Effect of Emotions on Health

The emotional brain responds to an event
more quickly than the thinking brain.
Daniel Goleman

Emotions - everybody has them. Some emotions are "good," or positive; and some . . . well, they're not so positive. No one goes through even a single day without feeling a range of emotions; in fact, some people seem to be *ruled* by their emotions.

You know exactly what emotions are; research indicates that they are universally experienced through all cultures. Some of the positive ones include happiness, excitement, satisfaction, pride, amusement, trust, and pleasant anticipation. Some of the not so positive ones include fear, anger, contempt, sadness, disgust, embarrassment, and shame.

You may figure you know all about them, since you experience them every day - but, believe it or not, scientists have been unable to agree on what emotions are and even how they should be studied. But even though scientists and researchers have a tough time defining exactly what emotions *are*, they do agree on one important thing: emotions have a significant impact on your health and well-being.

If everyone has emotions, why are they so difficult to define? Part of the reason is that emotions are complex reactions that involve the mind, the body, and behavior in a tightly constructed dance. Another reason they're so difficult to define is that everyone experiences emotions in different ways. You probably don't "feel" anger the same way your friend does; in fact, depending on a broad variety of factors, the same emotion may vary widely in the same person - you may "feel" anger as anything from mild annoyance to blinding rage and everything in between. Finally, emotions are hard to define simply because they're so hard to describe. If you don't believe that try asking a few people what falling in love "feels" like.

There's more: with a few exceptions, you usually can't tell by looking that someone is experiencing an emotion. (And you know those exceptions: the drooling student with the glazed-over eyes who seems ready to topple off the edge of her chair is clearly experiencing boredom. The parent who is yelling at you, spit spraying and veins bulging on his purplish-red neck and forehead, is clearly outraged at the way you handled his child.) Outside of those kinds of extreme emotions, you generally can't *see* emotions: the person experiencing them has to describe them to you. And the very process of describing them, as you know if you've ever tried, is anything but easy.

Make no mistake: just because you can't see an emotion doesn't mean it's not having an effect on your body. In fact, emotions cause some of the most dramatic impact possible on your health and well-being. There are lots of examples: engaging in a thirty-minute argument with your partner can slow your body's ability to heal by at least a day. On the other hand, expressing affection to that same person lowers your cholesterol. Love helps you grow new brain cells. Even *anticipating* laughter reduces the level of stress hormones. We'll go into the specifics a bit later.

Here's another thing you should know right off the bat about emotions: they are *not* the same thing as mood. An emotion is normally pretty short-lived but can be intense. Emotions are also likely to have a clearly identifiable source; they are specific reactions to very particular events. For example, if you get told that an initiative you've been fighting for all semester has been denied by the school board, you might feel pretty angry, disappointed, frustrated, or disgusted - or even a combination of those emotions - for a few hours (or even until you're able to soak in a hot bath with a favorite novel that night).

Your *mood*, on the other hand, is generally much milder than emotion but tends to last a lot longer. It's also a lot more difficult to identify the specific cause of a mood. You know the feeling: you totally get that you're in a grouchy mood, but you may not know exactly why.

The Three Components of Emotion
In their efforts to define *emotion*, most researchers agree that there are three components of emotion: feelings, physical responses, and expressive behavior.

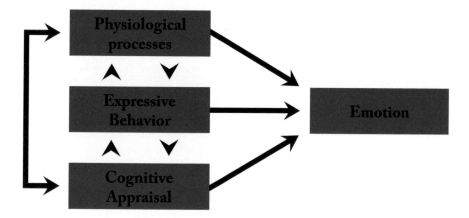

Have a positive attitude, high self-esteem, a strong sense of self, and the ability to recognize and share a wide range of feelings with others in a constructive way.

Feelings
People all over the world, regardless of culture or background, have the same *kinds* of feelings when they experience emotions. But those feelings vary tremendously in intensity and even in their very nature from one person to another - and even at different times in the same person. As a result, we recognize that emotions are very subjective - in other words, originating in and relating to the mind, so they're different for everyone.

That's easy to understand when you consider how differently you've experienced your own emotions. Think about sadness. Is all sadness the same? You can probably remember times when you've experienced sadness as anything from a touch of sorrow (reading in the newspaper that a woman was injured when a teenager ran a red light and struck the bicycle she was riding) to a sense of wretched despondency (learning that a troubled student with whom you've spent a lot of time committed suicide).

Most people often experience mixed emotions - a combination of very different feelings at the same time or in rapid succession. Imagine you have just received a prestigious new position in a prominent private school. You're likely to cycle through a variety of emotions ranging from excitement, anxiety, pride, nervousness, happiness, and maybe even a touch of fear.

Physical Responses

Just as the body responds in a very predictable way to stress, so the body has a very predictable response to intense emotion. Researchers have learned that no matter your age, gender, or race, your body responds to intense emotion (especially fear, panic, or anger) by releasing adrenaline (also called epinephrine). This hormone acts as a chemical messenger that causes very specific physical reactions, all of which can be measured.

Let's say you start experiencing an intense emotion. Regardless of what the emotion is, if it's intense enough your palms sweat; your heart pounds; your face gets flushed. You start breathing rapidly. Your muscles tense, and your tone of voice changes. You get restless. You might even faint. Many of these can be observed by people around you, though some can't be easily seen. At this point, epinephrine can be measured in your blood.

Recent research has shown a direct link between the brain and emotions. Brain imaging has shown that intense emotion activates the amygdala, a tiny almond-shaped structure in the brain that fuels physiological responses to emotion. Studies show that the amygdala is particularly active when a person experiences fear.

Expressive Behavior

Here's the component of emotion that's probably most familiar to you, because it's the part you can actually *see*. In most cases, this is where you can tell that someone else is experiencing anything more than a mild emotion - you'll see it in her body language or in his facial expressions.

Many behavioral expressions of emotion are pretty universal. For example, someone who is happy usually smiles; his eyes light up. You can literally see happiness written all over a person's face. On the other hand, someone who is experiencing intense sadness may cry, frown, furrow her forehead, wring her hands, or cover her mouth with her hand. And someone who is angry may clench his jaw, frown, ball up his fists, speak loudly, and have a flushed face.

Many of those behaviors are universal. Someone who is smiling is almost certainly feeling a positive emotion - such as happiness, love, joy, excitement, or amusement - no matter his age, gender, or cultural background. But various cultures can have an impact on how emotions are expressed. For example, Dutch people tend to interpret someone's emotion by watching facial expression; Japanese people, on the other hand, interpret emotion by how the voice sounds. The *preference* of emotion also differs based on culture, say researchers: Europeans prefer excited smiles and emotions, while the Japanese and other Asians prefer more calm expression of emotions. In some Asian cultures, it is considered improper to express certain emotions, such as disgust, anger, or fear.

As we mentioned, regardless of what researchers do and do not know about emotion, they all agree on this: emotions have a significant impact on health and well-being. In fact, at their extreme, emotions can have one of the most dramatic impacts possible on health and immunity. There are many ways that positive emotions contribute to both psychological and physical well-being. In the same way, negative emotions play an important role in the development of certain physical and psychological problems; they include emotions like anxiety, anger, aggression, and depression. In addition, consistent negative emotion has a major harmful impact on the immune system.

When our emotional health is in a bad state, so is our level of self-esteem. We have to slow down and deal with what is troubling us, so that we can enjoy the simple joy of being happy and at peace with ourselves.

Jess C. Scott

Positive Emotions and Health

Nobody is happy *all the time*. In fact, nobody has any positive emotion *all the time*. Does that mean you will permanently forfeit the benefits of positive emotions? Absolutely not! What's important is that you *regularly* respond to situations in your life with positive emotions. The occasional burst of anger, surge of sadness, or rush of fear may have a temporary effect, but if your *usual* response is a positive one, you'll experience tremendous health benefits.

And here's the good news: evidence shows that if you repeatedly respond in positive ways and with positive emotions, the structure of your nerves literally undergo physical changes that will cause them to habitually respond in a positive way. Barbara Fredrickson of the University of Michigan says it's a habit worth developing and that certain positive emotions - including joy, interest, contentment, pride, and love - may be very distinct, but they all share the ability to imprint your system with positive responses. In other words, the more you cultivate and experience positive emotions, the more your body will naturally gravitate to them.

And there's more. The part of your brain involved in attitudes and emotion is directly "wired" to your immune system. What that means is this: when you experience positive feelings and emotions, you stimulate your immune system. And a healthy immune system helps you resist illness and heal faster if you do get sick.

Finally, if you cultivate positive emotions and a positive outlook, you'll be much better equipped to handle negative things when they do come along. Like a rubber band, you'll bounce back no matter how far you are stretched or pulled by negative circumstances.

Optimism

You know what optimism feels like: you see the glass as half full, not half empty. You experience positive feelings. Most of the time, you expect a positive outcome, no matter the current circumstances. You believe that you can make a difference in how things turn out. You have hope.

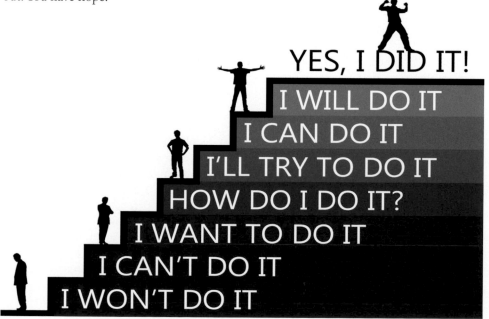

As it turns out, optimism has tremendous influence on the immune system. In fact, it sends "live" messages to the body and literally kicks the immune system into gear, promoting the healing process. And that has been a consistent finding of more than five hundred scientific studies conducted over a period of more than thirty years: nurture optimism, and you'll have a far stronger immune system. Of all the emotions, optimism seems to have the strongest ties to healthy immunity.

Optimism can even increase your ability to resist infectious diseases. A fascinating study at West Point identified cadets who had the Epstein-Barr virus, the culprit responsible for infectious mononucleosis. As it turned out, only about one-fourth of the cadets who were infected with the virus actually got sick. The ones who stayed healthy had a few important things in common - including consistent optimism, which fueled and strengthened their immune systems.

Want to increase your optimism? Try some of these exercises:

- Get a simple journal and use it to help you identify the things you can feel optimistic about. Every day, write down three things in your life that went well that day, and explain why. Over even a short period of time, you'll start to see what's going great, and you'll have reasons to feel more hopeful and optimistic.
- Identify and comment on things that cause you to feel positive. When a waitress gives you particularly good service, stop and talk to the manager on your way out, giving a few specifics about the excellent service. When the custodian goes above and beyond the call of duty to clean up a difficult mess in your classroom, write him a note of appreciation.
- Go for a walk in your area a few times a week, and take your cell phone or a camera.
- Snap a photo of each thing you see along your path that is interesting, unusual, or funny.
- Within your belief system, find something you can do to increase your belief about the higher purpose and meaning of life.
- Make it a habit every day to express your gratitude for the good things that happen in your life.

A sense of belonging and connection to other people appears to be a basic human need—as basic as food and shelter. In fact, social support may be one of the critical elements distinguishing those who remain healthy from those who become ill.

Kenneth Pelleteir

Love

We're not talking here only about romantic love, though such love does play a role in good health. When we say *love*, we're talking about your connection with other people - your ability to experience intimacy, attachment, and support through a network of people to whom you feel close.

Let's start with the most basic facts: we know that people with strong social contacts - a spouse or partner, a close-knit family, good friends, and church or other social contacts - have better health and live longer. Those who are isolated and unable to form loving contacts with other people have poorer health and die earlier.

A great deal of research has been done on the social ties that foster love. There are several ways in which the love that accompanies social ties protects health. First, it leads to an overall positive feeling and sense of self-esteem and control, all of which have been shown to protect health. And it is also an important buffer against stress, which protects you from stress-related diseases.

One specialist in infectious disease commented that real people contend with a type of "battle stress" every single day, and that "people who have a close-knit network of intimate personal ties with other people seem to be able to avoid disease, maintain higher levels of health, and . . . deal more successfully with life's difficulties." Some have gone so far as to call close social relationships and the love they engender a "safety net" against a wide variety of diseases.

I keep my mind focused on peace, harmony, health, love and abundance. Then, I can't be distracted by doubt, anxiety, or fear.

Edith Armstrong

Again, a main reason for this protection goes back to the immune system. Healthy social ties - even a few close family members and friends - improve immune function, help you resist disease, and enable you to heal more quickly if you do get sick. One big reason for that is the fact that stress deals a major blow to immunity, but love and social ties actually *reverse* the adverse effects of both short- and long-term stress. Simply put, your immune system is stronger and better able to function even when you are experiencing stress.

Spirituality

You may associate "spirituality" with the church to which you belong or a system of religious beliefs that govern your behavior. In actuality, *spirituality* is a set of complex feelings or emotions that cause you to search for the ultimate meaning of life. (That search is often achieved through religious organizations, though the feelings that prompt it are a deeper set of emotions.) The emotions associated with spirituality are based on inner experiences, individual growth, and the vision for limitless possibilities.

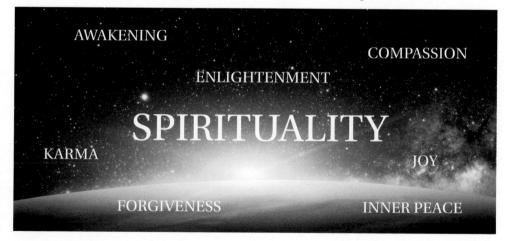

Spirituality gives meaning or purpose to life, produces great pleasure, leads to happiness, and encourages a sense of selflessness and a willingness to give of self to others (altruism). It entails a commitment to God or a higher power and results in a set of principles or ethics by which to live. It may include prayer or other experiences that reflect spiritual awareness.

Numerous studies demonstrate that spirituality has a profound influence on both physical and mental health. Part of that may be because spirituality is directly linked with hope, faith, commitment, an internal sense of control, enhanced self-esteem, and a sense of connectedness with others - all factors that we know improve health and boost immunity. Spirituality enables us to find meaning and purpose in life, even when we are struggling with crisis. As such, it protects us against the effects of stress.

One researcher described a woman who had been imprisoned in a concentration camp for most of her youth and who had seen most of her family tortured and killed. Of her, he remarked, "She had every reason to be weak, bitter, sick, and depressed. Instead, she was one of the most joyful, hardy women I have ever met." That strength, he said, was due to her astonishing spirituality.

Those who experience the emotions connected to spirituality are able to rise above their circumstances and find opportunities to lift, strengthen, and care for others. Their pain is significantly reduced. They are able to resist disease. They go to the doctor far less often. They have far less cancer. Their risk of depression is dramatically reduced. They bounce back much more quickly from illness. Their immunity is better. In fact, researchers from Harvard University found the link between good spiritual health and good physical health "striking."

One of the major emotions involved in spirituality is forgiveness - the ability to release past hurts and offenses, something one researcher calls a "process of healing." One of the most healing aspects of forgiveness is that it releases you from a cascade of negative emotions - among them anger, hostility, fear, and guilt - that we know to harm both health and immunity.

Forgiveness can be learned. Several tools can help you learn the skill of forgiveness and avoid the harmful health effects associated with failing to forgive:

- Admit that the feelings you are struggling with stemmed from events that really happened.
- Realize that the past cannot be undone. You can move forward with hope for a better tomorrow, but there's no such thing as a better yesterday.
- Accept others for who they are, not for who you want them to be.
- Release any unrealistic expectations of others and yourself.
- Realize that someone you forgive may not respond to your efforts to forgive; the important thing is not how that person feels, but how you feel.
- Try to be more flexible about the "rules" you have for others and yourself.

Negative Emotions and Health

If you're human, like everyone else on this planet, you've felt your share of negative emotions - depression, sadness, worry, fear, anxiety, grief, anger, and hostility, to name a few. When your heart starts sending negative emotions to your brain, the result looks chaotic and irregular, and your body interprets those signals as stress - something sure to cause problems.

We know with certainty that negative emotions pack a real punch to health and longevity. But here's the important thing to remember: *occasional* episodes of negative emotions are not what makes you sick or cripples your immune system. The problem comes when you experience *chronic* episodes of negative emotions - you're almost *always* worried, almost always anxious, almost *always* angry.

Face it. When you're in your new car, running behind on your way to an important district meeting, and you get rear-ended by an aggressive or careless driver, you're going to feel some anger. You might even throw in some worry (what's going to happen if I'm late?) and some anxiety (how much of this damage will my insurance cover?). But when you straighten all that out, good health dictates that you'll return to your generally happy, satisfied, calm self.

When experienced chronically or to excess, all negative emotions are dangerous to your health - but the emotions discussed below are particularly devastating.

Negative Emotions and Health

Most of the worries you worry about never happen!

Anger
Weakens the liver

Grief
Weakens the lungs

Worry
Weakens the stomach

Stress
Weakens the heart and brain

Fear
Weakens the kidney

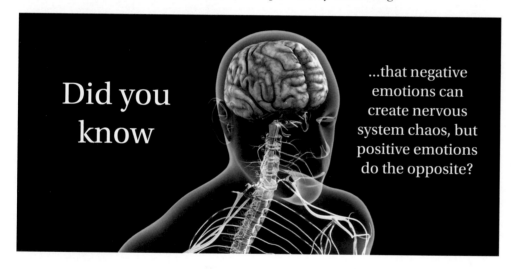

Did you know ...that negative emotions can create nervous system chaos, but positive emotions do the opposite?

Depression

In the short term, *depression* is a normal human emotion that can be caused by conflict, trauma, loss, or anything that disrupts the normal balance of your life. Depression can also be a side effect of certain medications or physical illnesses. A second kind of depression, not caused by emotion, is a clinical and biological illness that is based on chemical abnormalities in the brain; in that case, the pleasure centers in the brain are shut down, and everything in life seems bad.

Depression is not a sign of weakness. It means you have been strong for far too long.

If you don't think your anxiety, depression, sadness and stress impact your physical health, think again. All of these emotions trigger chemical reactions in your body, which can lead to inflammation and a weakened immune system. Learn how to cope, sweet friend. There will always be dark days.

Kris Carr

People of all ages and in all walks of life suffer from depression. It affects both genders, though it is twice as common among women (and no one seems to know why). A number of famous people - including Abraham Lincoln, Winston Churchill, and Ernest Hemingway - have suffered from depression, which Churchill called "the black dog." Short-term depression is often unavoidable, and if it resolves relatively quickly, does not result in damage to the body. The problem occurs when depression lasts for months or even years - and that's the kind of depression we're talking about in this chapter.

It's pretty obvious that depression has a profound effect on the mind and the emotions, but it has an equally profound effect on the body. During depression, the body undergoes the same cascade of changes that it does during chronic stress. And here's the really bad part: when depression is present, the stress response loses the ability to "turn off." Cortisol and the other harmful stress hormones keep pumping out and circulating through the body. And that's no minor thing: these stress hormones create structural changes in the brain, including the parts of the brain responsible for thinking and memory. The longer the depression persists, the more these areas of the brain shrink.

Be smart enough to know when you need help and brave enough to ask for it.

And that's not all: people who are depressed *seem* to be almost lethargic, when in fact the stress hormones coursing through their veins cause them to be in a constant physical state of high arousal - something that has crippling results. The response of the brain to this excessive activity in the body causes even more devastating effects: there is a shutdown of the parts of the brain involved with thinking, decision making, and controlling automatic defense mechanisms. The brain chemicals that help relieve pain are shut down; the result includes migraines, chronic pain disorders (such as fibromyalgia), arthritis, and even PMS. Pain is actually magnified.

Finally, depression impairs the immune system in a variety of ways.

Long-term depression can even shorten life. One obvious reason is that depression can lead to suicide. But another is that depression increases the likelihood of developing medical diseases that can be deadly - things like stroke, heart attack, sudden death syndrome, certain cancers, Parkinson's disease, diabetes, kidney disease, and epilepsy. Research shows that depression even shortens the survival time of people who are already ill.

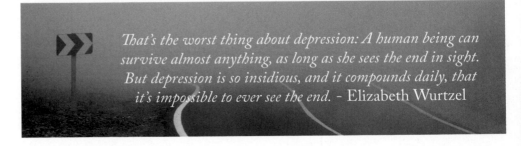
That's the worst thing about depression: A human being can survive almost anything, as long as she sees the end in sight. But depression is so insidious, and it compounds daily, that it's impossible to ever see the end. - Elizabeth Wurtzel

Worry, Fear, and Anxiety

At first glance, worry, fear, and anxiety seem like almost the same emotion. In actuality, though, there are important differences between the three.

Fear is probably the easiest to define; it's an emotion that occurs in response to an external threat; you usually react by trying to escape or avoid the threat. *Anxiety* is a little more difficult to define: it's an emotion that occurs in response to a *perceived* threat that you think you can't control or avoid. There's a big difference: fear occurs when you are confronted by a grizzly bear on your favorite hiking trail. Anxiety occurs when, without any concrete evidence, you are convinced your contract will not be renewed. An estimated 15 percent of the population experiences what's called an *anxiety disorder*, characterized by excessive worry about a number of things (instead of a single specific situation) more than half the time for a period of at least six months. Physical symptoms of an anxiety disorder can include chest pain, back pain, dizziness, heart palpitations, numbness or tingling, and trouble swallowing.

Worry is the interest you pay on a debt you may not owe.

Keith Caserta

Then there's *worry*, an emotion that is much milder than either anxiety or fear. It's a preoccupation with *potential* danger or pain. Worry is your attempt to mentally cope with your fears and concerns. Worry isn't always completely bad; for example, it can be positive if it helps you become more vigilant (watching for signs that grizzly bears have been spotted in the area) or helps you take steps to keep something negative from happening (doing a better job so your contract will be renewed). Too often, though, worry is no more than a destructive use of energy that, instead of helping you avoid disaster, actually causes you to visualize failure instead.

Again, it's all a matter of frequency and duration. Occasional fear is normal; after all, how else are you supposed to feel when confronted by a grizzly bear? So is occasional anxiety; everyone faces situations perceived to be potentially dangerous. But when you're

The secret of health for both mind and body is not to mourn for the past, not to worry about the future, or not to anticipate trouble, but to live the present moment wisely and earnestly.

Buddah

feeling worried, fearful, or anxious much of the time, those emotions can have profoundly harmful effects on your health and immunity.

Fear has a pronounced effect on the body: the heart races, the head spins, the palms sweat, the knees buckle, and breathing becomes labored. It's much like what happens during stress - and as with stress, the body can't endure it for long. The most marked effect of fear is on the heart: blood pressure spikes and the heart pounds; both rate and strength of the heart's contractions increase. If the fear is intense enough or prolonged enough, all body systems overload and death results. And a sudden surge in the hormones associated with fear can literally cause someone to be "scared to death" when the hormones immediately damage the heart muscle (this is the phenomenon that caused deaths from voodoo curses in the Caribbean). Medical history is full of examples of people who were literally frightened to death. One man even died of fright as he stepped up to a podium to deliver a speech.

Here's the difficult part: the physical effects of fear are exactly the same whether the fear is completely understandable or totally illogical. Your heart will be battered to the same degree whether you are being charged by a grizzly bear or walking up to the podium to give a speech.

Chronic worry overworks the nervous system and literally wears it out. It does the same to the immune system and the endocrine system (responsible for hormones), leading to a state of chronic stress. It also causes physical changes in many of the body's systems that lead to physical illness. And the power of worry is intense: Chronic worry is literally the visualization of an imagined catastrophe, and it's powerful. If you constantly worry about experiencing more physical pain, for example, the neurotransmitters throughout your body physically change so that you will, indeed, have more pain. (The opposite can also happen!) In other words, the brain has the ability to cause *physical changes* that create the very things about which you've been worrying.

In a number of studies, worry has also been shown to cause high blood pressure: it causes contraction of the arteries leading to the skin, muscles, intestines, and kidneys. Significant increases in blood pressure result. And it has been strongly associated with asthma; worry causes the body to produce the chemical acetylcholine, which constricts the airways. Worry causes muscles around the bronchioles in the lungs to become so tight that air cannot flow through them. Finally, worry actually triggers spasms in the airways, causing or worsening asthma.

Anxiety also has a significant effect on the body. While only about 15 percent of the general population suffers from extreme anxiety, researchers at the University of Utah and UCLA medical clinics found that half of those coming to the clinics suffered from anxiety and almost as many had significant depression. Here's what that means: more than half of the physically ill people are coming from the 15 percent of the population that's anxious.

Worry and anxiety have a particularly devastating effect on the heart and circulatory system; those who are worried and/or anxious have a 40 percent higher risk of heart attack. And once someone suffers a heart attack, worry can be especially harmful: those who worry excessively about their heart condition are significantly more likely to develop the kind of irregular heart rhythm that leads to sudden cardiac death.

There are a few things you can do to help overcome worry and anxiety:

- When you start to feel worried or anxious, slow your breathing. Breathe deeply in and out, focusing on the fact that your worry and anxiety are just thoughts as you let the breath flow out of your mouth.
- Make a plan to solve problems. If you're feeling worried or anxious about something that is coming up, make a clear and workable plan to deal with the situation. If you're worrying about something that may not happen at all, imagine the worst possible scenario, then work out a plan to deal with that.
- Change your way of thinking. It's not the situation that stresses you, but the way in which you think about the situation. Try to look at things more clearly and maturely.

Anger and Hostility

Anger and *hostility* are often considered the same, but they're actually quite different. *Anger* is a combination of *temporary* physical and emotional arousal. The key word here is temporary - it comes and goes. It can range in severity, depending on what provokes it. It may or may not be accompanied by physical or verbal expressions; when it's suppressed or bottled up, there is generally no outward expression of anger. You can easily identify what has made you angry.

Hostility, on the other hand, is not a temporary emotion; instead, it's a long-term attitude. An ongoing accumulation of anger and irritation, it is the repeated expression of anger in an aggressive way. Anger can be motivated by a student who consistently disrupts class in a negative way. Hostility, on the other hand, is much broader in scope; it is motivated by animosity and hatefulness and is usually associated with a suspicious and cynical view of the world. Sometimes, hostility is connected with clinical depression. It comes from the Latin word *hostis,* which means "enemy"; to the hostile person, everyone is an enemy - the person in the checkout line, on the freeway, in the elevator, at work, in the house next door. Eventually, a hostile person becomes his or her own enemy. The most dangerous kind of hostility is *free-floating hostility,* an attitude in which one is angry or on the verge of anger *all the time*. It takes surprisingly little to make such a person snap.

Holding on to anger is like grasping a hot coal with the intent of throwing it at someone else; you are the one who gets burned.

Buddha

Anger and Hostility

Hostility is not the only means of misdirecting anger.

Anger not channeled consciously comes out in all sorts of ways.

- being silent (passivity or avoidance)
- being negative and sarcastic
- exaggerate being upset over trivial irritations
- getting other people upset (to relieve one's own anger).

Get mad, then get over it.

Colin Powell

Anger is an acid that can do more harm to the vessel in which it is stored than to anything on which it is poured.

Mark Twain

Anger was valuable to our early ancestors; as they experienced the fight-or-flight response, a little dose of anger helped them either fight or flee with great strength. Today, in contrast, we are expected to behave calmly and rationally as we deal with problems. While research has shown that it's actually healthy to express anger, we're expected to do it in a healthy, managed way.

The health effects of prolonged, repressed, or chronic anger are diverse, widespread, and devastating. To get an idea of how anger affects the body, check out the results of a questionnaire given to several thousand people asking how they felt when they were angry: they described pounding heart, nosebleed, dizziness, tears, mottling of the face, headaches, snarls, or even the complete inability to vocalize at all. Much of what happens during anger is the same thing that happens during stress - heart and breathing rates speed up, blood pressure soars, digestion slows down, and muscles tense up. And the same hormones are released, causing all the same health problems as caused by stress.

Anger beats up the immune system, too. In one study, people who were angry were significantly more likely to get sick when exposed to viruses that cause the common cold. But there's more: they were much more likely to get sick if they simply *talked* about anger.

One of the most pronounced effects of anger and hostility is on the heart and circulatory system. The emotion of anger itself can directly create angina and heart attack. In fact, the American Heart Association says that people who tend to explode in anger during an argument double their risk of heart attack, especially in the two hours after the argument. Among those with lower education, that risk *triples*.

Heart disease is significantly higher among people who are frequently angry. But the danger multiplies when the anger is suppressed. Men who are unable to express their anger in appropriate ways have a 75 percent higher risk of developing heart disease. The risk for women is similar.

Hostility has an even greater impact on the heart than does anger alone; in fact, it is a leading factor in heart disease risk. In one study, more than 80 percent of hostile men had seriously diseased coronary arteries, and the risk was even higher for hostile women. Hostility shreds the lining of the blood vessels, causes abnormalities in the wall of the heart muscle, decreases the amount of blood pumped out by the left ventricle, increases cholesterol, and dramatically increases the risk of heart attack and coronary artery disease.

Hostility also increases the risk of vascular brain disease, dementia, insulin resistance, metabolic syndrome, and cancer.

Chronic anger has also been linked to some types of cancers; in particular, women who have difficulty expressing anger have a significantly higher risk of breast cancer. Other studies have shown that suppressed anger in women also impacted the survival rate of cancer patients; those who were able to express anger survived longer. Interestingly, men who consistently *expressed* anger died from cancer much more rapidly. Overall, suppression of anger in both genders predicted higher death rates, especially from cardiovascular disease.

If you struggle a bit with anger, consider using these tools to help:

- You've probably heard this all your life, but it works: When you feel like you're about to lose control, step back, take some deep breaths, and count to ten. Not only will you get a new perspective, but the act of deep breathing helps slow down your system.
- When you start feeling angry, look for better ways to view your situation. Ask yourself, *Would a really wise person react to this situation the same way?* Again, just stopping for a minute to think and breathe will start to slow things down, and you're likely to discover a new perspective. As a bonus, look for a humorous aspect in what you're facing.
- If another person is the cause of your anger, try forgiveness.
- When you start to feel angry, stop and do something soothing instead. Listen to a favorite piece of music; close your eyes and envision something you love (the climbing rose in full bloom across your trellis); stroke your pet. You get the idea: do whatever it takes to distract yourself from the thing that's making you angry. Giving yourself some time to step away will probably help you think of some better ways to react.

What about hostility? There are also some effective tools that can help with hostility as well. Since hostility is not as situational as anger, you need to work on some overall attitudes:

- Realize that when you let other people make you angry or hostile, you're giving all of your power to them. Stop doing that. Own your emotions, which is the first step to controlling them.
- Practice laughing - especially at yourself. Laugh at situations, but not at others. You'll be surprised to find out how funny the world is.
- Play some fun games, both alone and with others. The goal is not to win; the goal is to relax and have fun. Making connections with other people is a bonus.
- When things don't go the way you want them to, give yourself permission to stay calm. So what if you have to change plans or strategies? The world won't end!
- Practice smiling at other people. You don't need an excuse; just do it!
- At least three times a day, compliment someone. Be genuine. As you practice, you'll find lots of things to admire about people, which will help reduce cynicism and suspicion.
- Volunteer to help people who are less fortunate, which can help you connect to others in a healthy way. There are a myriad of opportunities in most communities.
- Look for chances to honestly say, "Maybe I'm wrong." Then believe it. There's nothing wrong with being wrong - and admitting it helps take the fuel out of hostility.
- Practice speaking calmly, slowly, and without using obscenities. Even if you're angry, focus on keeping your tone of voice calm and peaceful.
- And here's one that several leading researchers have suggested: Pretend that today is your last day. If it truly was, you wouldn't want to waste a shred of energy on being mad.

Chapter 5

The Importance of Social Support and Relationships to Good Health

Chapter 5
The Importance of Social Support and Relationships to Good Health

A sense of belonging and connection to other people appears to be a basic human need – as basic as food and shelter. In fact, social support may be one of the critical elements distinguishing those who remain healthy from those who become ill.
Dr. Kenneth Pelletier

One of the best things you can do for your health is also one of the easiest - and, for that matter, one of the most pleasant: surround yourself with people you love! If that comes as a surprise to you, check out what one of the most comprehensive studies on social support revealed: people with strong social contacts - a spouse, a close-knit family, a network of good friends, an affiliation with people in a club or at church - had better health and lived longer.

Those results held up even after all kinds of factors were considered. Regardless of their gender, ethnic background, race, or socioeconomic status, the people who had a strong social network were healthier and had longer lives.

Contrast that with the people who were isolated. As you might guess, they had poorer health and died earlier. In fact, they died at rates as much as five times higher than did the people who had good social ties. We'll explore the reasons why in a minute.

As we talk about the impact of social ties, it's important to remember that there are no guarantees, and everyone undoubtedly knows an exception to the rule. But remember too that what science has proven gives us something we should seriously think about. "Some well-loved people fall ill and die prematurely," the researchers concluded; "some isolates live long and healthy lives. But these occurrences are infrequent. For the most part, people tied closely to others are better able to stay well."

What Is Social Support?
So what, exactly, is *social support*? Simply stated, it's the degree to which your basic needs are met through your interaction with other people. It's the network of people who help you cope with stress and who provide intimacy and attachment to you.

There are four different kinds of support that the people around you provide:

- Tangible help or services that help you when you need it. This is the kind of support provided by someone who cares for your children every Wednesday when you have a meeting after school or who pitches in to help rake the leaves from your impossibly massive maple tree. Imagine that you've gotten ill or undergone surgery: a person who provides tangible support is the one who drives you to your doctor's appointment, does your laundry, cleans your bathroom, or brings you and your family dinner.

The world is so empty if one thinks only of mountains, rivers, and cities; but to know someone who thinks and feels with us, and who, though distant, is close to us in spirit, this makes the earth for us an inhabited garden.

Johann Wolfgang von Goethe

- Emotional support that includes love, empathy, caring, and trust. When you're ill, this is the person who holds your hand and provides love and encouragement.
- Advice, suggestions, and information that can help you make decisions or deal with new or challenging situations. This is the person who suggests a list of questions to ask your doctor or who brings you an informative brochure on the resources for dealing with the disease with which you have just been diagnosed.
- Appraisal, feedback, and support that can help you more accurately evaluate yourself or succeed in self-improvement efforts. This is the person who suggests a great new exercise routine and offers to be your fitness partner.

Sometimes the same person can provide all four kinds of support. In other cases, various people in your life can fill different roles when it comes to providing the support you need.

Okay, so the term *network* can seem a bit daunting. What kind of numbers are we talking about here? That all depends on you! Some people need a large, diverse system of people in order to feel a secure connection to people. Others need a much smaller circle of friends who are reliable and with whom they experience the intimacy of a very close friend.

Research has shown that in order to provide significant support, your social ties need to provide six things to you:

- A sense of belonging
- A sense of personal worth along with a sense of being valued and esteemed
- A feeling of being loved and cared for, including an opportunity for shared intimacy
- Shared communication, companionship, and obligations
- Access to physical assistance
- Access to advice, guidance, and information

You might be thinking, *That's all well and good, but who on earth has the ability to spend meaningful time with a huge network of people?* Well, here's the good news: no matter the size of your social network, you don't actually have to spend time with them or even get help from them to benefit from their support! The benefits come from just knowing they are there and that you *can* turn to them for support if you need to.

Before we move on, let's make an important distinction: *social support* is not the same as a *support group* (such as Alcoholics Anonymous, a support group for breast cancer patients, or a support group for victims of crime). Support groups are structured groups that provide self-help meetings usually run by a mental-health professional. Social support comes from the people in your life who provide you with a sense of esteem, value, belonging, and love - the people you can turn to for help of any kind.

My friends and family are my support system. They tell me what I need to hear, not what I want to hear, and they are there for me in the good and bad times. Without them I have no idea where I would be and I know that their love for me is what's keeping my head above the water.

Kelly Clarkson

Some people enter our lives and leave almost instantly. Others stay, and forge such an impression on our heart and soul, we are changed forever.

Author Unknown

To be isolated is the greatest tragedy for a human being and the most generic form of stress.

Joan Borysenko

Social Isolation and Loneliness

A 2011 study found that loneliness can lead to more frequent sleep disturbances.

A 2009 study published in health psychology found that you are less likely to be physically active if you are lonely.

A 2012 Harvard study round that middle aged adults who live alone have a 24% greater risk of dying of heart disease.

A 2013 study at Ohio State University found that loneliness, like chronic stress, strains the immune system.

A University of Chicago study found that loneliness can increase your levels of the stress hormone cortisol which can lead to depression or even stroke or heart attack. other digestive problems.

One more thing is important to understand: the kind of social support that most benefits health is generally not derived from a single person or relationship. The most powerful effects of social support come from an accumulation of relationships (across the spectrum or over time) that provide affection, nurturance, love, and other positive emotions. The higher the number of these sorts of relationships you have over time, the greater the benefit to your health. In the same way, a single or isolated relationship that creates stress, isolation, or other negative effects in your life is not likely to harm your health; destructive health consequences generally come from repeated patterns of stress, isolation, and other negative elements.

The Harmful Effects of Loneliness and Isolation

We know that loneliness can have devastating health consequences and can even shorten life. We'll talk about that in greater detail in just a minute. Until then, know this important fact: Many associate *loneliness* with *being alone*, but there are actually important differences between the two.

Loneliness is a condition in which you feel disconnected or isolated. You may feel defective or different in some way; you may feel unloved, useless, or misunderstood. You may feel that you can't develop or don't have satisfying relationships with other people. Notice the common word in all those descriptions: *feel*. Loneliness is a *feeling*, which means it may be a little different for every person who experiences it. It's not a *condition* - in fact, you can feel miserably lonely in a crowd. Loneliness can strike people of any age, gender, ethnicity, race, education, or income level.

Loneliness is *not* the same as being alone. The hallmark of loneliness is lacking a sense of satisfaction from relationships with other people. Someone who lives alone and is alone much of the time may not feel lonely at all if she derives great satisfaction from the relationships she does have. (Additionally, many who live alone actually enjoy their "alone time," which they spend developing creative talents or enjoying hobbies.) On the other hand, someone with hundreds of friends or other social ties may feel incredibly lonely if she is unsatisfied with the connection she has with those friends.

Causes of Loneliness

There seems to be an upward trend toward loneliness in the United States. As just one piece of evidence, researchers conducted a survey in 1984; those surveyed most frequently reported that they enjoyed three close confidants. When the poll was repeated twenty years later, most of those surveyed reported having no confidents at all.

The numbers tell a sad story. Experts estimate that one in five adults in the United States feels lonely at least once a month - and that one in ten struggle with loneliness at least once a week. There are a number of reasons for increasing numbers of the lonely as well as a handful of risk factors.

As mentioned, living alone doesn't necessarily cause loneliness, but it can contribute to the factors that eventually lead to loneliness. U.S. Census figures show that more people than ever are living alone - an unprecedented 27 million. Contributing to the risk of loneliness are trends away from marriage, increased divorce rates, and smaller size of average household. Another contributor is the increase in mobility: almost half of the U.S. population relocates in any five-year period, and with relocation comes the challenge of establishing new social ties.

Some of the risk factors for loneliness include:

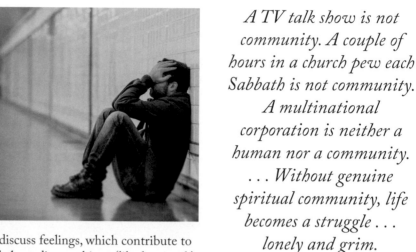

- **Age.** Most at risk are the elderly (those over eighty) and adolescents. The elderly face tremendous losses through the death of a spouse, siblings, and friends, and many face the additional burden of relocation and the challenge of establishing themselves in a new neighborhood or community. Teenagers, while often very socially active, tend to have unrealistic expectations of friendship, leading to a lack of satisfaction.
- **Gender.** While women are more likely to admit they are lonely, women also are more prone to develop deep, intimate relationships and to remain friends over long periods of time. Women are more prone to discuss feelings, which contribute to intimacy in a relationship, while men are more likely to discuss things (like last week's football game). In addition, men tend to make fewer friends as they get older.
- **Marriage.** Those who are happily married tend to be the least lonely. Next come those who are single and have never been married. Those who are widowed or divorced generally are the most lonely and are at higher risk for social isolation, more pronounced hopelessness, lower emotional support, and more frequent depression.
- **Family structure.** Families in which the parents are lonely tend to create an antisocial family unit in which at least some of the children isolate themselves and repeat the patterns they learned in the home.
- **Income.** Economic restrictions among low-income people often result in far fewer opportunities to socialize.

Others at particular risk for loneliness include students changing schools, children of divorcing parents, people who are moving, people who are starting a new job, people who are unemployed, people who have a chronic or terminal illness, and prison inmates. Among the loneliest people are college freshmen, who have left behind family and friends and who are trying to adjust to a completely new situation. Some studies indicate that fully half of all loneliness may be due to genetics.

> *A TV talk show is not community. A couple of hours in a church pew each Sabbath is not community. A multinational corporation is neither a human nor a community. . . . Without genuine spiritual community, life becomes a struggle . . . lonely and grim.*
>
> David James Duncan

The eternal quest of the individual human being is to shatter his loneliness.

David James Duncan

Loneliness is the greatest unrecognized contributor to premature death in the United States.

James J. Lynch

The Health Consequences of Loneliness
The isolation that accompanies loneliness is such a significant risk factor for illness and death that scientists have compared its importance to obesity, a sedentary lifestyle, and maybe even cigarette smoking.

The biggest disease known to mankind is loneliness.

You don't have to experience loneliness for years in order to be impacted by it. Both short-term and chronic loneliness are major risk factors for illness and premature death from a variety of causes. In fact, those who are socially isolated are twice as likely to die earlier than those with strong social involvement. Apparently the effects of loneliness accumulate over time, contributing to the wear and tear of stress and aging on the body and actually speeding up the process of aging. In fact, a Harvard University specialist says you can tack an automatic fifteen years onto your life just by reducing two factors, one of which is loneliness.

Hundreds of in-depth studies demonstrate that chronic loneliness, social isolation, and lack of human companionship are among the leading causes of premature death. A host of studies place the risk of premature death among the lonely at twice the rate of those who aren't lonely. Among women, the risk is three times higher.

What should young people do with their lives today? Many things, obviously. But the most daring thing is to create stable communities in which the terrible disease of loneliness can be cured.

Kurt Vonnegut

While loneliness is a significant risk factor in a wide variety of illnesses, it plays a particularly devastating role in death from heart disease. Researchers at Duke University Medical Center studied a group of people with coronary artery disease for five years; only 17 percent of those with a spouse or close friend (or both) died during the five years, while 50 percent of those without a spouse or close friend died. Studies show that even after factors like age, family history of heart disease, cigarette smoking, and physical inactivity are taken out of the picture, *loneliness alone* increases the risk of dying from cardiovascular disease by 40 percent.

So what does loneliness do to the heart? A number of studies have shown that there is an actual physiological link between loneliness and heart disease. Loneliness causes changes in the nerves and endocrine system that lead to atherosclerosis. One researcher said that the impact of loneliness on blood pressure is "stunning" - as much as inactivity or obesity - especially in those over the age of fifty. And that's not all: loneliness compounds the effect of stress on blood pressure - but only among women.

We know that loneliness increases the risk of death and almost all kinds of disease. The reason seems to be the impact of loneliness on immunity. Loneliness is an actual stress, and it kicks off the stress response, complete with all the stress hormones, which we know cause all kinds of negative effects on the body. Those stress hormones affect every cell in the body and significantly impact immunity. The result? Loneliness can make you sick, keep you sick, and interfere with your ability to get better. It can even increase the amount of pain you feel.

Tests have shown that lonely people secrete an excessive amount of the stress hormone cortisol - a hormone that suppresses immunity. And that's not all: loneliness apparently affects the way you are able to cope with stress. People who are lonely may not suffer more stress than others, but they recall more of it later, seem more threatened by the stress, are more helpless in the face of stress, identify more sources of stress, and are less likely to ask for help. They also seem to develop chronic stress much more readily, with steady amounts of epinephrine circulating through their bodies. Those steady levels of epinephrine keep them in a chronic heightened sense of arousal. Simply put, loneliness inflicts significant wear and tear on the body, including the immune system.

An Important Word of Caution

If you've decided that it's time to improve your social connections, choose living, breathing human beings - not people you hook up with on social media sites like Facebook.

Yes, it's tempting to simply reach out and click a few buttons to end up with a list of hundreds of "friends" - but those generally aren't the sort who will drive you to your doctor's appointment or rake your leaves or hold your hand while you're moaning and groaning from the flu. Are these the people who will meet your basic needs? Almost certainly not.

There's nothing wrong with having "friends" on social media. But one of the nation's leading researchers on loneliness says that if you use Internet connections as a *substitute* for physical connections, all those virtual "friendships" will actually *increase* your feelings of loneliness. And two new studies suggest that superficial relationships - the kind you cultivate on social networking sites - actually *increase* feelings of detachment and have been shown to dramatically increase disease risks. In other words, they won't do you any good if you're trying to improve your social ties.

What it all boils down to is this: weak relationships, even in massive numbers, will make you feel more isolated and lonely. When it comes to the kind of strong relationships that improve your health and well-being, the important thing is *quality*, not *quantity*.

The Effect of Social Support on Health

By now, you should understand quite a bit about what social support is. You also understand that Facebook and other social media sites aren't the best place to drum up social support - not the good kind, anyway. So before we delve into the dramatic benefits of social support on health and longevity, let's look at some good sources of social support.

Social support can actually come from all sorts of places: your spouse, family members, friends, neighbors, coworkers, other professional associates, and people who belong to the same church, club, professional associations, or fraternity as you do. Another great source

Heroes were ordinary people who knew that even if their own lives were impossibly knotted, they could untangle someone else's. And maybe that one act could lead someone to rescue you right back.

Jodi Picoult

of social support are volunteer associations - you can grow very close to people who volunteer and spend their time in the same cause you do.

Importance of Social Support

Purpose and meaning
Live longer
Increase self-esteem
Less anxiety and depression

Various factors play a role in social support. One of them is gender. For example, the main source of social support for married men is their wives. Not so with married women: they rely more heavily on other family members and friends than they do their husbands. And social support is known to encourage and promote positive health behaviors (like exercise and avoiding substance abuse), but only among women.

Another factor is age. You might think that the elderly benefit the most from the social support they receive, but studies show that's not true. A national survey revealed that the elderly benefit most from the social support they *contribute* to their network, not what they take from it.

Still another factor is income - but it appears to be a *perceived* factor instead of an actual one. There is a set of fairly universal stressors that accompany low socioeconomic status, things like crowded living conditions, financial strain, distrust of others, and even fear of increased crime. While these stressors are very real, the reduced social support that results from them is actually only *perceived* to be lower.

Across the spectrum, one of the most important sources of social support is belonging in a neighborhood - and the important word is *belonging*. The very feeling of "belonging" dramatically reduces the risk of loneliness. A neighborhood provides a number of health-promoting factors, primarily the act of neighbors pulling together to make positive changes and help each other out. When people feel as though they belong in a neighborhood, they are less likely to move, something that also reduces the risk of loneliness. A number of studies have shown that a strong sense of belonging to a neighborhood reduces stress (a health benefit all on its own), improves mental health, increases the likelihood that people are physically active, and improves mental health. And that applies to people of all ages; in fact, a strong sense of belonging in a neighborhood is particularly important in promoting both the mental and physical well-being of children.

How Does Social Support Protect Health?

Believe it or not, we don't have a good answer to that question. A myriad of studies have been done proving that social support definitely protects health and promotes longevity - but as to *how* that happens, there is no definitive answer.

There *are* a number of theories, and many of them are standing up to close scrutiny. Some think it's because strong social support creates a sense of good self-esteem, an overall positive feeling, a sense of stability, and feelings of control, all of which increase the ability to cope with stress. Some think it's because strong social support itself acts as an actual buffer against stress. Still others think social support engenders a feeling of control, which we know leads to better health. And research shows that strong social support is strongly linked to good health behaviors and fewer risk-taking behaviors.

Whatever the reason, strong social support is also linked to robust immunity, an obvious contributor to health and longevity. Research has conclusively proved that disrupted or interrupted social connections suppress the immune system. In fact, when such a disruption occurs early in life (such as a child being separated from a parent), the impact on the immune system can last two years or longer.

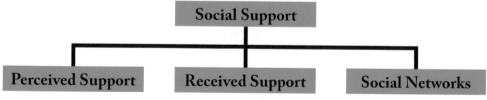

There's also the notion that strong social support is a "vast untapped resource" when it comes to providing a very real type of health-care support. Fewer than 5 percent of all physician visits are for psychological problems, even though most of them are directly related to physical problems. But, points out a professor of Duke University's School of Medicine, we "learn that if we want a doctor's attention, we must focus on a physical symptom. A woman might tell her doctor she has a bladder infection," but she'll tell a friend "that she's lost her job, had a fight with her husband, and has a bladder infection." She says that "the great majority of human ills are never seen by a doctor. The real primary care is provided by one's family, close friends, and neighbors."

That phenomenon is closely tied to confiding, which researchers believe may have the greatest impact on health. One of the top researchers in the field points out that confession is actually liberating and dramatically relieves stress. In fact, the health benefits associated with confiding to a family member or close friend can last as long as six weeks.

The Health Benefits of Social Support

We may not know exactly how it happens, but experts across the spectrum wholeheartedly agree that something very important is happening when it comes to social support. "The ties that bind," as they are so often called, are also the ties that help us live a long and healthy life.

People who have a close-knit network of intimate personal ties with other people seem to be able to avoid disease, maintain higher levels of health, and in general, to deal more successfully with life's difficulties."

Leonard Syme

One study in Michigan that spanned a period of ten years found that people with weak social ties had a suppressed immune system. Those same people had much higher rates of cancer, coronary heart disease, strokes, arthritis, upper respiratory infections, and mental illness. A separate study conducted by the U.S. Office of the Surgeon General found that strong social support kept troops in World War II from collapsing from battle stress, and that strong social support enabled the troops to withstand even intense battle stress. And that's not all: members of small combat groups that enjoyed the strongest social support were also the ones who suffered the lowest casualties.

Other studies show that those with strong social ties get sick far less often, have lower serum cholesterol levels, are far less prone to depression, and are significantly more healthy, even in the face of substantial stress (such as unemployment). In a study of pregnant women who were under dramatic stress, only 33 percent of those with strong social support developed complications in pregnancy despite the level of stress they endured. In sharp contrast, 91 percent of those with weak social support developed complications during the pregnancy.

Countless studies have all shown the same thing: those who have strong social support enjoy stronger immunity and better health across the lifespan.

Social Support and Longevity

The results of a number of studies show that those who live longer are those who surround themselves with at least a few people who can act as friends and confidants. That finding has proven true in every study across the board, no matter how the studies are set up or who is included in them. In fact, a group of almost 150 studies involving more than 300,000 people show that those with stronger social relationships have a *50 percent* increased likelihood of living longer.

The effect of social support is so robust that doctors and research teams have used it to accurately predict who was still going to be alive at two-, five-, ten-, and fifteen-year follow-up visits. Those who enjoyed a strong network of social support are still going strong.

One study that involved more than three thousand adults showed that strong social support is so protective that it delays natural declines in health by as long as a decade. Researchers who conducted the study felt that the influence of social support in predicting health and disease is as powerful as well-known risk factors, including cigarette smoking, alcohol, obesity, and physical inactivity.

In fact, social support is such a powerful factor in prolonging life that it even lowers death rates among those who are *already unhealthy*. When researchers studied more than 2,500 elderly people who had been hospitalized for heart attack, the effect of social support was absolute. Among those who said they had no source of social support, 38 percent died while in the hospital; of those with one source of social support, the figure fell to 23 percent. Contrast that with those who reported stronger social support: only 12 percent of those with two or more sources of social support died in the hospital. The researchers concluded that "being married or unmarried, living with someone or living alone, are not as critical to surviving a heart attack as just having someone to turn to for emotional support. And this support seems to act like a drug - the higher the dose, the greater the protective effect."

The reason social support contributes to long life is the same reason it promotes good health: social support improves immune function. The opposite is also true: a lack of social support - characterized by things like a small or weak social network, marital difficulties, divorce, bereavement, loneliness, or stressful social relationships - batters the immune system. The result is not only poorer health, but an increased risk of death.

Another reason why social support promotes health and longer life is that it actually *reverses* the adverse effects of both short-term and long-term stress. We know that stress is a major factor in health and longevity, and that's all linked up to immunity too. Stress cripples the immune system and reduces the body's ability to fight off illness. Researchers have now found that a strong social network of good interpersonal relationships protects the function of the immune system *even in the face of stress*.

One researcher who did a ten-year study of breast cancer patients found that the role of social support was "much greater than anything I expected." He and other researchers determined that those who did the best were those with social support - and those that did the most poorly had feelings of hopelessness and isolation. The same types of results have been duplicated in vast numbers of studies involving patients with all kinds of cancers, heart disease, stroke, and diabetes.

Happy Marriage, Healthy Life

While married couples make up the smallest percentage of American households in more than two centuries, and the number of unmarried women in this country has surpassed the number of married ones, the facts are in: having a happy marriage dramatically increases the chances of good health and long life.

While the relationship between marriage and health is more complex than originally thought, study results are conclusive - happy marriages provide the greatest benefits of

A good marriage is good for you. That isn't just a platitude. Mounting research shows that it is the literal truth. When your marriage is healthy, your body and mind are healthier."

Cliff Isaacson

Happy Marriage, Healthy Lifestyle Rules for a Happy Marriage

Never both be angry at the same time.

Never yell at each other unless the house is on fire.

If one of you has to win an argument, let it be your mate.

If you have to criticize, do it lovingly.

Never bring up mistakes of the past.

Neglect the whole world rather than each other.

Never go to sleep with an argument unsettled.

At least once everyday try to say one kind or complimentary thing to your life's partner.

When you have done something wrong, be ready to admit it and ask for forgiveness.

It takes two to make a quarrel, and the one in the wrong is the one who does the most talking.

both health and longevity. That's partly because of the social support offered by the marriage, but it doesn't stop there. Being married generally boosts social support from other sources as well: those who are married are usually better integrated into the neighborhood and community and normally have a much easier time establishing a strong social network. In fact, researchers agree that the entire spectrum of social networking is enhanced and made easier by marriage.

Marriage also provides other factors that play a role in better health and longevity. For example, many married people have an economic advantage, some with double incomes; those who are married are at lower risk of being below the poverty line. Married people are also most likely to have health insurance. Another is that married people tend to have better health habits, maybe because they are accountable to someone else in the house - they tend to eat better, exercise more regularly, see a doctor for regular checkups, visit a physician if they suspect something is wrong, and be more compliant with medication.

People who are happily married enjoy a number of health benefits: they have lower rates of cancer and heart disease, improved sexual fulfillment, better overall physical and mental health, and - possibly most important from a health point of view - stronger, more robust immune systems. As far as immunity goes, marriage appears to have a significant effect on strengthening and protecting the immune system. And the better the marriage, the better the immune function.

In fact, there is only one area in which happily married people are not better off: obesity. Married men are particularly prone to be overweight or obese, with the greatest problem among middle-aged men (75 percent). Those who have never married are the least likely to be obese.

But before you run out and get a marriage license in an effort to cure all your woes, listen carefully: the health and longevity benefits of marriage apply to those who are *happily* married. Single people have the second-best health and longevity benefits when it comes to marital status. Following the singles are those who are separated, divorced, and widowed. And bringing up the rear are those who are *unhappily married* - they suffer the worst health and greatest risks to health and longevity.

The potential fallout of an unhappy marriage - divorce - also brings with it potential health and longevity problems. Every major study shows that those who are divorced suffer more physical and mental problems than those who have been single their entire life. And research shows that divorce has the same impact on health as smoking a pack of cigarettes a day. Those who are divorced have higher rates of cancer, heart disease, high blood pressure, pneumonia, and accidental death than those who are married, single, or widowed. And researchers have figured out why: it appears to be because divorce removes an important source of social support - not only the former spouse, but family members and friends as well.

Want to strengthen your social ties? Try some of the following suggestions:

- Tell people that you want to improve your social connections. When people know you're interested, they'll help by making introductions, among other things.
- As you begin to make friends, don't overwhelm people. Keep initial contacts genuine but brief. Keep things positive and be sure to respect boundaries.
- Listen. People love talking about themselves, and you'll have greater success making and keeping friends if you are genuinely interested in them.
- Make a plan for what you'll be doing a year from now, five years from now, and so on. Don't rely only on your colleagues at work as your social network - when you retire or quit, you'll need other sources.
- Find a cause you're committed to, and volunteer. Not only will you improve your social connections, but volunteering brings health benefits all its own.
- Consider community causes, religious activities, or political campaigns. Look for groups to join whose members share your interests. Look for professional organizations or groups offered in your community or through your church.
- Consider taking a class through community or adult education. Choose something in which you're interested or a skill you'd like to learn, such as flower pressing, cooking ethnic cuisine, or painting.
- You might also consider going back to school for an advanced degree. If you decide not to pursue a specific degree, you might consider taking classes in which you're interested but you didn't have time to take while you were getting your degree - classes like anthropology, early European history, botany, or Swedish genealogy. Check out the offerings at your local community college or university; you'll be stunned as to the variety of subjects you can take.
- If you have a pet (which can be a great source of social support in itself), look for others who share your love of pets. For example, if you have a dog, start visiting a local dog park, then strike up conversations with the people you meet there.

- Join a gym, fitness facility, or other exercise group. The exercise itself is a proven way to reduce stress. Even better is making friends with others who attend. If you can't find a group that fits in with your schedule, organize your own! For example, start a walking club in your neighborhood, at your school, or among members of your church congregation.
- Work on developing a healthy self-image. If you fall at either extreme - vain or arrogant at one end, constantly fearful and self-critical at the other - you will not be especially appealing to potential new friends.
- Avoid the tendency to complain, especially at first. Keep a positive outlook, and bring along your sense of humor. Someone who is constantly complaining and whining drains everyone's energy.
- Forget trying to compete. If you're always considering others as rivals, you close the door to friendship.

Chapter 6

How Spirituality Affects Your Health

Chapter 6
How Spirituality Affects Your Health

*The secret of health for both mind and body
is not to mourn for the past, not to worry about
the future, or not to anticipate troubles, but
to live the present moment
wisely and earnestly.*
Buddah

When we say that spirituality has a significant effect on your health, your mind probably makes the soaring leap to religion - the church to which you belong. That's spirituality, isn't it? Not exactly - and it's not what we're talking about here. While there *are* some similarities between religion and spirituality, there are some pretty considerable differences too. So before we discuss this important aspect of health, let's make sure we're all on the same page regarding exactly what we're talking about.

What Is Spirituality?

In defining spirituality, let's start with religion. The word *religion* comes from the Latin word *religio*, which describes the bond between man and a greater power. You're probably most familiar with it as something that describes the relationship between man and God. Religion generally includes particular doctrines, ecclesiastical practices or systems, and certain rituals; "organized" religion comes from grouping these doctrines and rituals into specific religions or churches. These churches generally dictate or encourage certain beliefs and behaviors among their members.

*Whenever you hear or read
anything of a spiritual
nature that moves you or
touches your soul, you are
not learning something . . .
you are remembering what
you have always known. It
is a gentle awakening.*

Meenu Rathore

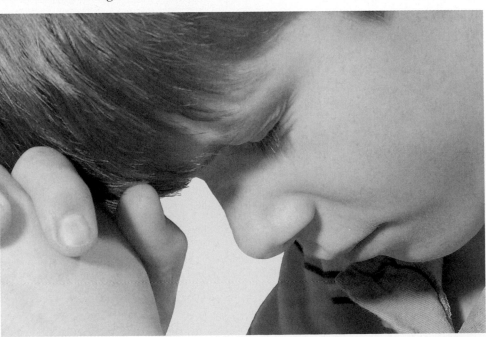

Religion is often the way people express, expand, or practice their spirituality. But religion is *not* spirituality.

What, then, is spirituality? The word *spirituality* comes from the Latin word *spiritus*, which means "breath," "life," or "source of life." It describes the connection between man and all sources of life: a divine being, the earth, the environment, the cosmos, nature, animals, or other human beings. Spiritual health or well-being involves achieving oneness with all sources of life and focusing on the energy of life that invites healing and wholeness.

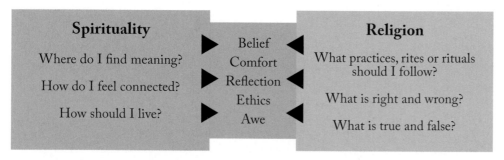

Spirituality	Belief	**Religion**
Where do I find meaning?	Comfort	What practices, rites or rituals should I follow?
How do I feel connected?	Reflection	What is right and wrong?
How should I live?	Ethics / Awe	What is true and false?

Spirituality is the cornerstone of religion, but spirituality is *not* religion.

Spirituality and Religion: How Do They Differ?

As we mentioned, there are a number of similarities between spirituality and religion - but there are also significant differences:

- Spirituality focuses on individual and integrated growth; religion focuses on creating a community.
- Spirituality is universal and emphasizes unity; religion is particular and segregates one group of people from another (the Catholics from the Protestants, for example).
- Spirituality is feeling-based and focuses on inner experiences; religion is behavior-based and focuses on outer, observable practices.
- Spirituality is difficult to identify and measure; religion is fairly easy to identify and measure (how often do you attend church?).
- Spirituality is an intensely individual experience; religion involves formal behaviors, specific worship practices, precise direction, and explicit doctrine that all members of a church are expected to practice and with which they are expected to comply.
- Spirituality creates vision and the power for possibilities; religion provides a practical form by which to realize a vision or possibility.
- Spirituality is most often associated with individual experience; religion is most often associated with elements of institutional and ritual practice.

This is not a good versus bad situation - spirituality, with its many dimensions, improves your health, increases your resilience, and boosts your immunity. We'll talk all about that in a minute. But so does religion; in fact, regular participation in a religious congregation

Spirituality does not teach us to run away from everyday life issues and problems. It is a training to pass through the difficulties and issues and face it bravely. It helps us to become whole and to behave efficiently. Spiritual life is a practical life.

Satish Kaku

Spirituality speaks from the soul. Religion speaks from the mind.

Anthony Douglas Williams

Religion is a bridge to the spiritual - but the spiritual lies beyond religion.

Meenu Rathore

is one of the factors that leads to better health and improved longevity. So don't bury your church activity in the bottom drawer - or, worse yet, take it out with the weekly trash. Just make sure you embrace the benefits provided by spirituality along with any church activity you enjoy.

The Spiritual Dimension of Health

Spirituality has been a recognized part of wellness throughout all of recorded history, and it continues to fascinate researchers and practitioners in all areas of medicine. In fact, it is an important dimension of health, along with the physical, mental, emotional, and social dimensions, which we've already discussed. Too often, the spiritual dimension of health is virtually swept under the rug and is too rarely considered as part of the whole person when it comes to health and well-being.

Today, increasingly more practitioners are recognizing the importance of spirituality in the overall scheme of wellness, and researchers are starting to paint a much clearer picture of what has been vaguely known for millennia. One researcher wanted to define not only spirituality, but the spiritual dimension of health - and in her quest to come up with an accurate definition for both, she interviewed a wide range of people who worked in the health and medical fields - including, among others, health professionals, health educators, and health students. After gathering all the data, she determined that the spiritual dimension of health:

- Gives purpose or meaning to life.
- Is a set of ethics or principles by which to live.
- Includes a commitment to God.
- Is recognized by us intuitively but is not easy to explain to others.
- Includes a sense of selflessness, a willingness to give of ourselves to others, and an altruistic feeling toward others.
- Creates within us a perception of what causes the universe to work the way it does.
- Is the part of us that produces the greatest amount of pleasure.

Combining the results of her interviews with a lot of additional research, she identified four aspects of spiritual health. It is spiritual well-being, she says, that convinces us we can survive and brings us pleasure, even in the most difficult situations. According to her in-depth analysis, she believes the spiritual dimension of health:

- Is based on your faith and perception that there is a higher power at work in your life.
- Creates or brings into focus the meaning of life - a vital aspect that gives you the will to live. That particular "meaning of life" may differ dramatically from one person to another. For example, you may find your greatest meaning in humanitarian efforts and your commitment to help others. Or your greatest meaning in life may consist of your family relationships, which are the most important thing to you. Still others may find their greatest meaning in professional contributions and accomplishments, such as in touching the life of a student. Whatever your meaning of life, it's essential; without it, you lose your will to live.
- Acts as a unifying force that brings the other dimensions of health together into a unified whole.
- Goes beyond the limit of the individual to create a common bond among people. The spiritual dimension enables you to share love, compassion, and warmth with the other people in your life - you are able to move beyond yourself to do unselfish things in the service of others.

Spirituality [is] the domain of awareness where we experience values like truth, goodness, beauty, love and compassion, and also intuition, creativity, insight and focused attention.

Deepak Chopra

While spirituality can be generally difficult to identify, certain behaviors can indicate spirituality. These include things such as regular prayer, a sense of closeness to a higher being, a clearly defined meaning or purpose in life that guides behavior, a sense of closeness to other people, meaningful contemplation, and other experiences that indicate spiritual awareness.

Though you may not have thought much about it, your spirituality has a pretty profound impact on many of the decisions you make every day - even without church membership or participation. Some of the decisions and subsequent behaviors that are affected or even directed by your spirituality include what kind of music you listen to, what kinds of movies you see, what kind of books and other media you read, whether you use drugs or alcohol, your decisions regarding organ donation, and the degree of sexual intimacy in which you engage.

For something you may not have thought a lot about, your spirituality has likely played a major role in your life.

The Positive Effect of Spirituality on Health

Spirituality can and does have an influence on physical health - and that influence is often dramatic. The reason why can be attributed to the traits that come along with spirituality: love, faith, hope, a sense of purpose, and commitment, all five of which lead to good health through an internal locus of control, enhanced self-esteem, and a sense of connectedness (to others and to a higher power).

The results of a number of studies show that spirituality is associated with life satisfaction, marital satisfaction, and a sense of well-being, all of which have been shown to enhance the immune system and contribute to health. And the results of more than a hundred studies show that the practices associated with spirituality (such as prayer, contemplation, and meditation) reduce pain, anxiety, and depression. Spirituality also reduces the production of stress hormones - those culprits that can impact immunity and make you sick. In fact, the meditation associated with spirituality actually improves brain *structure* as well as *function*.

Researchers at UCLA, among others, have found that spirituality actually reduces pain, and they've figured out several reasons why. First, spirituality acts much like an antidepressant in significantly increasing serotonin output - and one of the "side effects" (a good one!) of serotonin is pain relief. That's not all: vivid spiritual experiences raise the levels of dopamine, another chemical produced by the brain that reduces pain and increases pleasure. Some of the other things associated with spirituality - meditation and commitment to something in which you intensely believe - calm the nerve transmissions involved in pain and have been shown not only to ease the pain associated with many common illnesses (such as headache), but to reduce chronic pain.

One researcher studied the lives of top business executives and other prominent people who had achieved real success. One of the chief things they had in common was a set of strong spiritual values and beliefs. Interestingly, many of them had suffered major physical or psychological trauma early in life, and their spirituality seemed to give them the ability to thrive and cope with the resulting stresses that often deliver a blow to health. That ability continued to help them throughout their lives.

Spirituality lies in what you do and how you do it and not what result you get.

Kapil Dev

How can health be without spirituality? The spiritual powers within lift all of humanity.

Bruno Cortis

Spirituality's Effect on Our Health

When a person feels they have a meaning and purpose, strength in their faith and hope = mental and physical well-being.

If an illness or injury arise; spirituality assists with recovery or coping with illness, as it motivates, enables, and empowers the patient. Decreases in blood pressure, cholesterol, and depression may occur.

WHO has concurred that spirituality is the '4th dimension' to health, completing and complementing the physical, mental, and social aspects to a person as a whole.

Spiritual Wellness

Find meaning in life events, demonstrates individual purpose, and live a life that reflects your values and beliefs.

Spirituality seems to have a powerful effect on all dimensions of health because of the sense of purpose and meaning it brings. One well-known example comes from Viktor Frankl, a Jewish survivor of a Nazi prison camp who became an astute observer of what went on among his fellow prisoners. His classic book, *Man's Search for Meaning*, said that the prisoners who did the best in the worst of conditions were those who demonstrated spirituality through a sense of purpose and meaning. They were the ones who saw their situation in the camp as an opportunity to lift, strengthen, and care for their fellow prisoners - something that gave them a purpose for being there. Frankl demonstrated his own spirituality when he proclaimed that his captors could control his circumstances, but they could not control his attitudes or the way in which he reacted to those circumstances.

The same kind of thing has been found among hospitalized adults. Even those with terminal illness have much stronger emotional health if they also have a high level of spirituality. Those who are the most spiritual have been found to experience less discomfort, feel less loneliness, have less fear of death, and find a greater emotional adjustment to their situation. Those with terminal cancer and other serious illnesses find that their spirituality gives them a much more positive perspective on death.

Researchers at the University of Maryland Medical Center have found that spirituality helps people heal faster from surgery. It also reduces blood pressure, anxiety, and depression and helps people cope better with chronic illnesses such as heart disease, cancer, diabetes, arthritis, and spinal cord injury.

One of the aspects of spirituality that seems to have a significant impact on health is prayer. By definition, prayer is any psychological activity - conscious or subconscious, uttered or unspoken - that puts you in closer contact with the transcendent, including a divine power. Prayer involves all kinds of things that boost health, including love, empathy, hope, gratitude, and a sense of being blessed by the prayer.

Numerous studies show that prayer has powerful physical effects on the body. Chief among those is the fact that prayer kicks in the "relaxation response," a scientifically measurable response that causes real physical changes in the body. It slows down metabolism, reduces blood pressure, lowers the heart rate, slows breathing, and even causes brain waves to be less active. It also significantly reduces distress. According to the cardiologist who identified it, the relaxation response has "most often and effectively been elicited through forms of prayer."

Many of the health effects of prayer are likely due to the fact that during prayer, you are being physically still, clearing your mind of unnecessary thoughts, focusing on your deepest values, experiencing hope, figuring out ways to grow, feeling connected, and drawing on a power greater than yourself to help you solve your problems.

Whatever the actual reason, researchers agree that the prayer born of spirituality provides substantial benefits to physical and emotional health.

Faith and the Placebo Effect

One of the major aspects of spirituality is faith - and one of the most striking demonstrations of faith and health is the *placebo* effect, the physical change that occurs as a result of what we simply *believe* a pill or procedure will do. A *placebo* is generally a pill or tablet that is made of nothing more than saline solution, distilled water, or sugar. That's right: there is no actual medication in a placebo. But consider this: about one-third, and sometimes more, of all sick people respond well to a placebo - something they *think* is medication. When the person gets better from taking a placebo, the healer is faith, not medicine.

Placebos work because they rely on faith, a key component of spirituality. The anticipated response - what the patient *expects or believes* will happen - is so powerful that it affects neurotransmitters, which facilitate communication among the nerves. Those neurotransmitters in turn communicate to the body organs and systems. They turn on the brain functions that suppress pain; the placebo's impact on serotonin and dopamine is so powerful that it works as well as taking an opiate painkiller. Brain scans have shown that placebos cause the same changes in the brain as do the drugs they are meant to replace.

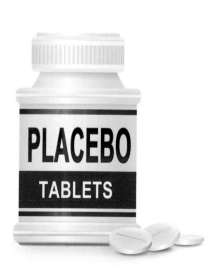

Most of the medical experiments that demonstrated the power of faith and placebos would not be allowed today because of laws requiring that patients be completely informed about all medical procedures being performed. But the studies done several decades ago provided substantial proof regarding the power of faith and the placebo - proof that still holds up today.

One of the most classic studies of the placebo effect was done in 1950 in a New York hospital with a group of pregnant women who were suffering severe nausea and vomiting. Doctors gave the women medicine they claimed had been proven to relieve nausea and vomiting. But without knowing it, the women were given syrup of ipecac, a drug

There are only two ways to live your life. One is as though nothing is a miracle. The other is as though everything is a miracle.

Albert Einstein

that is used to *cause* vomiting. Here's what happened: the women's nausea and vomiting *completely disappeared* after they took the syrup of ipecac. In other words, their *belief* in the healing power of the medication was so strong that it actually counteracted the usual pharmacological action of the drug.

Another classic study from the 1950s showed that the placebo was effective even in surgery - cases when a patient is put under anesthesia and an incision is made, but no surgery is actually performed. During the mid-1950s, a surgical procedure was developed to help relieve the chest pain caused by coronary artery disease. In the surgery, called an "internal mammary artery ligation," an artery in the chest wall was tied off. The initial response to the surgery was enthusiastic - more than half of the patients reported relief of chest pain, did better on electrocardiograms after the surgery, and exercise tolerance improved. The surgery gained in popularity, and thousands of patients were requesting it.

Not all surgeons were convinced that the surgery was beneficial, so a group of them decided to test it using a placebo. They randomly divided patients who wanted the surgery into two groups. The first group got the artery ligation. The second group, without knowing it, was put under general anesthesia; the surgeons made an incision in the chest and sewed it back up without tying off the artery.

What happened? Results of the patients in both groups was almost identical - many, including those who had no surgical procedure done, had less chest pain, improved electrocardiograms, a reduced need of nitroglycerin for pain, and an increased tolerance for exercise. The surgeons found that surgery on the artery was often no better than a simple skin incision - and that the incision alone led to a dramatic, prolonged placebo effect.

In talking about the placebo effect, a former instructor at Harvard Medical School used the example of the woman with an issue of blood who touched the hem of the robe Jesus wore and was instantly healed. Jesus told her that her faith had made her whole. "After centuries of slow progress toward rational explanations of the physical world," the Harvard instructor said, "even scientists can at last begin to appreciate the truth of His assessment. We are entering a new level in the scientific understanding of mechanisms by which faith, belief, and imagination can actually unlock the mysteries of healing."

The Healing Power of Altruism

Altruism - a key component of spirituality - is the giving of yourself out of a genuine concern for the welfare of other people. It has been defined as "unselfish benevolent love" and comes from the French word *autrui,* which means "other people." Altruism involves help and service you give to others without expecting anything in return.

Altruism develops early in life; children as young as two years of age respond to people in distress by reaching out with a comforting touch, bringing a parent to help, or offering a favorite toy. It's a hallmark of virtually all of the world's religions and is practiced by people in all walks of life - even those who traditionally should be the recipients of altruistic acts. A large-scale survey showed that altruism is unrelated to financial status: people of all socioeconomic levels routinely demonstrate altruistic characteristics.

Many feel that altruism may actually be one of our earliest skills as a species, because it is necessary for reproduction and survival as a species. Some also feel that it is a key factor

---

Placebo Effect Necessary Components

Positive beliefs and expectations on the part of the patients

Positive beliefs and expectations on the part of the physician or healthcare professional

A good relationship between both parties

Dr. Christina Puchalski

I don't know what your destiny will be, but one thing I know: the only ones among you who will be truly happy are those who will have sought and found how to serve.

Albert Schweitzer

in the development and expansion of the human brain, and may be embedded in the brain structure. New research shows that altruistic behavior may actually originate from how people view the world rather than simply how they act in the world. As a trait, it is an important part of spirituality because of its relation to love, forgiveness, apology, and reconciliation.

What makes someone altruistic? Many researchers believe that altruism is an instinct, dating back to the time when hunters and gatherers lived in small groups and depended on each other for survival. Others believe that it is a trait shared by everyone to some extent and that human nature is basically social, not selfish.

Some researchers also say that altruism can be learned, depending on your social or cultural background, your sense of responsibility, your stage of moral development, and the particular situations in which you are called on to help. Others believe that altruism is part of a set of personality traits that enable people to reach out to others when fueled by commitment to principle, allegiance to their group, or empathy. One pair of researchers studied the "rescuers" who helped the Jews during the Holocaust and found that they often risked their own safety and even their lives to help others. People like these, studies show, usually view themselves as one with all humanity rather than acting only in their own behalf - a standard hallmark of spirituality.

Those who are altruistic tend to share three general traits:

- They have a positive view of people in general.
- They are concerned about the welfare of others.
- They take personal responsibility for how others are doing.

The couple who researched the rescuers during the Holocaust put it well when they pointed out that altruism is "not the providence of the independent and the intellectually superior thinkers but that it is available to all through the virtues of connectedness, commitment, and the quality of relationships developed in ordinary human interactions." For those who foster and nurture their spirituality, altruism is part of an overall set of traits that connect spiritual people to those around them.

How Altruism Improves Physical and Mental Health

Altruism is an obvious benefit to those on the receiving end. But it also has dramatic effects on those who provide the service. A broad array of studies shows that altruism and altruistic acts boost physical and mental well-being, happiness, health, and longevity. A massive study compared those who volunteered altruistically with those who did not. Those who exhibited genuine altruism had better physical health, were happier, suffered less depression, and had improved longevity.

Another study of almost two thousand women who regularly volunteered to help others found that the altruistic women rated their health as better than or as good as others their age. That's not all: the altruistic women experienced relief from depression as well as all kinds of physical ailments - including things as simple as headache to those as complex as lupus and multiple sclerosis - from the altruistic acts themselves.

Studies show that those who regularly engage in altruistic acts experience an improvement in their own physical ailments. These include a reduction in the

Use your voice for kindness, your ears for compassion, your hands for charity, your mind for truth, and your heart for love.

Those who bring sunshine to the lives of others cannot keep it from themselves.

James Matthew Barrie

symptoms of arthritis, asthma, lupus, and migraine headaches as well as the frequency of colds and flu.

Research shows that altruism activates emotions that protect health and reduce negative attitudes - such as anger and chronic hostility - that damage the body and lead to poor physical health. Another benefit of altruism is that it gives people the ability to affect change even in situations where they might otherwise feel powerless.

By helping others…we help ourselves.

A Yale University professor of public health said, "When you're a helper, your self-concept improves. You are somebody. You are worthwhile. And there's nothing more exhilarating than that. That can influence your health."

Every man must decide whether he will walk in the light of creative altruism or in the darkness of destructive selfishness.

The benefits extend to mental health as well. A number of studies show that those who render loving and caring service to others without expecting anything in return enjoy better mental health than those who don't perform altruistic acts. Research showed that low-income seniors who participated in the Foster Grandparents Program had more positive emotions and exhibited more stable mental health. They and other seniors who regularly gave altruistic service had greater satisfaction with life, fewer mental disturbances, and a stronger will to live.

In a large study of members of a specific church, those who demonstrated altruistic behaviors had better mental health. In fact, the study determined that altruistic service was a powerful predictor of positive mental health. And studies of adolescents involved in altruism showed that they had a wide range of emotions indicative of good mental health; they also had higher self-esteem, greater future aspirations, better motivation toward academic work, and were more likely to graduate from college, do well academically, and enjoy better physical and mental health even into late adulthood.

The Effect of Altruism on Immunity

One of the reasons why altruism has such an impact on health is its effect on immunity. A simple experiment conducted by Harvard psychologists showed what happens. Volunteers were shown three films. The first was a gentle film on gardening. The second was a Nazi war documentary. The third was a film about Mother Teresa, a documentary about the Nobel Prize-winning nun who dedicated her life to charitable work among the lepers, the poor, and the orphans in India's most poverty-stricken regions.

Both before and after each film, researchers measured the amount of germ-fighting cells in the saliva of each volunteer. These cells are an important indication of how well the immune system is working. There was no change in the measurement of immunity after the first two films. But after volunteers watched the film about Mother Teresa, the amount of the immune substance in their saliva rose sharply - even among the volunteers who said they dislike Mother Teresa. Merely *watching* altruistic service caused an actual physical change in immunity, something that can protect physical health.

The beneficial effects of altruism may be so powerful, says one researcher, that it may even slow down the inevitable deterioration of the immune system that normally happens as you get older.

The Stress-Reducing Effects of Altruism

Another reason why altruism improves health is the fact that it reduces stress - and you already know the devastation stress can wreak on the body. The emotions involved in altruistic service apparently decrease or sometimes even eliminate the effects of stress. That not only helps prevent disease, but aids in the healing process when injury or illness does occur. One expert in stress said, "Altruism creates a physiological response that makes people feel stronger and more energetic and that counters harmful effects of stress."

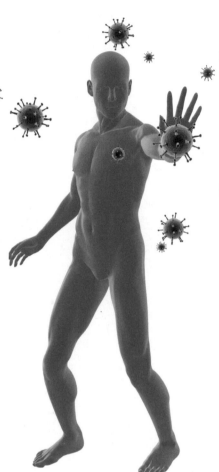

Psychoneuroimmunology

B lymphocytes fight bacterial infections, T lymphocytes attack cancer cells and viruses, and microphages ingest foreign substances. During stress, energy is mobilized away from the immune system making it vulnerable.

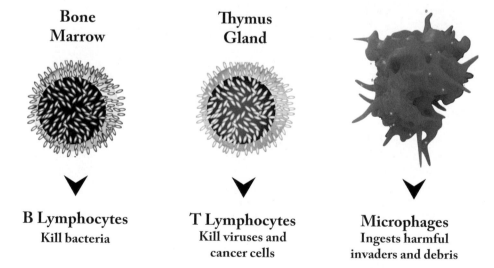

Bone Marrow	Thymus Gland	
⌄	⌄	⌄
B Lymphocytes **Kill bacteria**	**T Lymphocytes** **Kill viruses and cancer cells**	**Microphages** **Ingests harmful invaders and debris**

Remember the "relaxation response"? Researchers maintain that in addition to blocking some of the harmful effects of the stress response, altruism helps by *activating* the relaxation response, helping the blood pressure, heart rate, breathing rate, digestion, and hormone levels associated with stress return to normal. As one researcher put it, altruism combats the effects of stress by preventing nervous system "overload."

Altruism and Pain Relief

Ever heard of the "runner's high"? It's the phenomenon that creates a sense of well-being following exercise - a set of physical and emotional effects that have been described as feeling a type of "high." Well, guess what? Altruism has been shown to create a similar phenomenon called the "helper's high" - the release of endorphins that results from altruism acts as a natural painkiller and creates a sense of pleasure and joy. Researchers who have studied altruism note that it has the same benefits of enhanced well-being and reduced pain that people get from meditation and yoga.

The "healthy-helper syndrome," as a pair of researchers called it, actually consists of two stages. The first is a literal physical high - a "rush" of good feelings that are characterized by a sense of euphoria, warmth, and increased energy. These sensations are a result of the endorphins released by the brain, and they cause an immediate "feel-good sensation." The second stage is a longer-lasting sense of calm and emotional well-being. Together, the two provide a powerful antidote to stress, a way to combat depression and helplessness, and a boost of happiness and optimism.

The endorphins associated with altruism also act as a powerful painkiller - just as powerful, some say, as that associated with opiates.

Altruism and Longevity

In addition to all its health benefits, altruism also appears to improve longevity. Numerous studies show that those who participate in regular altruistic activities live longer - improving their lifespan by as much as one-third, according to some studies. The reasons why may include everything from increased immunity, better physical health, reduced stress, improved resiliency, and less loneliness and isolation. Regardless of the reason, the statistics are clear: those who regularly reach out to help others enjoy a longer and healthier life.

One of the most profound examples of the health and longevity benefits of altruism comes from the life of philanthropist John D. Rockefeller, Sr. Rockefeller entered the business world with gusto and drove himself so hard that by age thirty-three he had earned his first million dollars. Ten years later he owned and controlled the world's largest business. By the time he was fifty-three, he was the world's first billionaire. There was clearly no moss growing under this man's feet.

But Rockefeller's success came at a hefty price. The people he had crushed in his pursuit of wealth hated him; workers in Pennsylvania's oil fields hanged him in effigy, and he was guarded day and night by bodyguards pledged to protect his life. And when it comes to quality, it wasn't much of a life. His health took a massive hit. He developed alopecia, a condition in which hair falls out. His digestion was so poor that all he could eat was crackers and milk. He was plagued by insomnia. The doctors who struggled to help him agreed that he wouldn't live another year.

Then a miracle happened. John D. Rockefeller began to think of - and care about - others more than he did himself. He decided to use his billions of dollars for the benefit of others, and he expected nothing in return from any of them. He gave billions of dollars to hospitals, universities, missions, and private citizens through the Rockefeller Foundation. His generosity helped in the discovery of penicillin - and his monetary contributions to medicine enabled researchers to find cures for tuberculosis, malaria, diphtheria, and many other diseases that had robbed so many of life. In fact, his generous donations helped rid the South of its greatest physical and economic plague at the time: the hookworm.

When Rockefeller began using his riches to help other people, he actually helped himself as well. He felt renewed. For the first time in years, he was able to eat normally. He slept soundly. He defied the odds and lived to see his fifty-fourth birthday - and many birthdays after that. In fact, he kept on giving and caring for others until he died at the age of ninety-eight.

Five Spiritual Practices that Will Transform Your Life

Want to try incorporating more spirituality into your life? In his eBook *Live Free*, blogger Steven Bancarz suggests five practices that will bring increased meaning and spirituality into your life. Check them out and give these a try:

Practice 1: Stop and Take Ten Seconds

This one is stunningly simple. For some reason, your brain is convinced that it needs to think about your problems twenty-four/seven or else they won't go away. That's simply not true, and it becomes a significant source of stress. It's like a drug, and you're the addict. So start now to break the addiction: for just **ten seconds at a time**, refuse to think about your problem(s). Just ten seconds. Sit up and say, "For the next ten seconds, I am going to choose *not to think*." Then clear your head. Before long, it will become easier and easier to think of something else - something spiritual, if you will - most of the time, while dedicating some rational and concentrated thought to solving your problem.

Practice 2: Go into the Now

You know all those voices in your head? Make them be quiet *right now*. Instead of dodging all the chaos that's going on in your head, just be completely still and observe what's going on right now where you are. Focus on how your back feels against the chair. Really look at the light that's filtering through the window. Feel the air as it brushes against your arm. Hear the birds outside your window. Listen to the sounds of students out on the playground. Ask yourself how it feels to be inside your body. All those things are reality - and they are now. The past is a story, and the future is a possibility. All you really have is what's happening *right now*, so tune in to the present.

Practice 3: Choose Your Own Mental Activity

Do you realize that you can actually choose what you are thinking? Try saying a word out loud, then think about it; you might choose the word *dolphin, yellow, skirt, chalkboard,* or *Christmas.* Try it now: say it out loud, then think about it. It's really pretty easy, isn't it? Now realize that when you think something negative, *you have also chosen* that thought. Change it. You might be thinking, *I don't want to be teaching second grade this year. I don't know why the district didn't give me the sixth-grade class I wanted. I must be a loser.* Instead, choose to think, *I wasn't expecting to teach second grade again, but this will give me good experience. I'm learning new things and doing a better job. I'll be really prepared to make a move next year.* **You** choose the things you think.

Practice 4: Bring Consciousness to Each Action

There's a lot of misery-causing chatter going on in your head while you're daydreaming your way through life. You automatically walk out to your car in the morning; you automatically drive to school; and you automatically make your way to your classroom, daydreaming all the way. And all that time, a whole range of nonsensical babble is going on in your mind. Instead of just automatically going through the motions, bring every movement to conscious thought. Are you writing today's spelling words on the chalkboard? Feel your feet on the floor. How does the chalk feel in your hand? On what part of the chalkboard are you writing, and why? What does each word mean? Why did you choose that word? If some of that chatter tries to return, don't let it! Get into the practice of being present and aware of everything you're doing. Quieting the senseless noise will make you more receptive to the spiritual connections you're seeking.

Practice 5: Become the Witness

Bancarz says this is the biggest secret of all: No matter how much chaos is going on in your mind and how much pain it is causing you, you no longer have to participate in it. Instead of being the participant, become the witness. You are not your mind, and you are not the voices in your head. You are the space that surrounds all that, and you can retreat to that space for some peace. Just as a room is not the furniture that's in it, you are the space of consciousness, and not the objects in it. Take a deep breath. Look at the thoughts in your head. Witness them. Then look around. What's happening right now? Relax. This is the only moment that exists right now, and in this moment you are free to fill your life with the things that make up your spirituality.

Chapter 7

Three Essentials for a Healthy Physical Body

Chapter 7
Three Essentials for a Healthy Physical Body

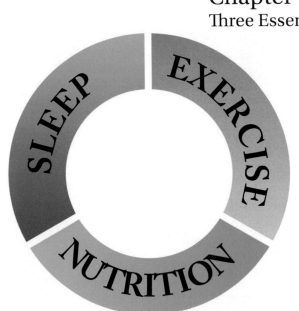

[Y] our body is talking to [you] all the time.
And please remember, your body loves you.
It does everything it can to keep you alive and functioning.
You can feed it garbage, and it will take it and digest it for you.
You can deprive it of sleep, but still it gets you up and running
. . . . It loves you unconditionally and does its best
to allow you to live the life you came here for.
The real issue in this relationship is not whether
your body loves you, but whether you love your body. . . .
It is time for you to . . . build a mutually loving relationship
with your own body.
Joshua Rosenthal

So far, you've learned a lot about how your mind and spirit affect your body - and vice versa. But when all is said and done, the foundation is a healthy body, and that relies on three essentials: good nutrition, regular exercise, and adequate sleep. A truly healthy body starts with having all three of those things in the right balance, and once you know the basics, it's not as hard to pull it off as it might seem.

How important are these three essentials? Consider this perspective: this is the only body you have. It's a one-and-you're-done deal. And it's the only place you have to live. So even though your body is extremely forgiving about most of what you do to it, it's worth doing whatever you need to do to take good care of it!

Balanced Nutrition for Optimal Wellness
If you think nutrition is important only to your physical body, think again - what you put in your mouth has a powerful impact not only on your body, but on your mind as well. We'll explain how a little bit later.

Before we talk about that and about how to make sure you're getting the right balance of nutrients, let's take a minute to look at the typical American diet. If you're like the vast majority of people in this country, you'll probably recognize a few of your own habits - and you're in good company.

The Typical American Diet Disaster
Experts across the board and from a variety of disciplines (all the way from nutritionists and dieticians to cancer researchers) have the same basic thing to say about the typical American diet: We eat too many calories.

Twenty-five years ago, the average American took in about 1,850 calories a day. Today, the average American eats at least 300 calories more than that. *So?* you might be saying. *That doesn't sound like all that much.* In a way, it's not - it's the rough equivalent of two cans of soda. But consider this: those extra 300 calories a day are enough to make you pack on *thirty-one extra pounds* every year. At thirty-one pounds a year, it doesn't take a genius to figure out that within not too many years, you could become fat. Really fat.

The food you eat can be either the safest and most powerful form of medicine or the slowest form of poison.

Ann Wigmore

And you wouldn't be alone. The Centers for Disease Control and Prevention recently came out with their latest findings - and as it stands, more than 68 percent of all Americans are overweight or obese (with a body mass index greater than 25). And as you might have noticed with your own students, childhood obesity has hit epidemic proportions over the last few decades. Experts point the finger at too much soda, too much high-fat food, and too little exercise - as well as kids who eat far too few fruits and vegetables. At the current rate of childhood obesity, it is predicted that today's American school children face a 33 percent lifetime risk of developing diabetes, with the number of diabetics in this nation increasing 165 percent by 2050.

When it comes to the typical American diet, there are two main culprits: junk food and fast food.

Let's start with junk food. The number-one source of calories in the typical American diet is sweets - you know them as cookies, cakes, pies, pastries, candy bars . . . you get the picture. Number four is soda. Not only do sweets and soda contribute far too many calories to the average diet, but they provide no nutrients. They are what the experts call "empty calories." Here's an alarming fact: the average teen gets almost 10 percent of his or her daily calories straight out of soda cans.

And what about fast food? You know how convenient it is, and America has an ongoing love affair with it. After all, there's a reason there are more than 170,000 fast-food restaurants in this nation - think of how many you pass on your way to school every day. Pair that up with more than 3 million soft-drink vending machines in the nation, and you can see how advertising and industry are adding to the problem - especially when there are fast-food restaurants and soda machines available in many public schools. Kids don't even have to cross the street to get them.

Physicians and scientists are so concerned about junk food and fast food that some consider these trends the new "tobacco" in terms of adverse health effects. Americans are

What the Government Wants to See

When it comes to what we're eating, the government is putting in its two cents' worth—but in this case, it's advice worth listening to.

Every ten years, the U.S. Department of Health and Human Services establishes health objectives for Americans, and they're not shy about what they would like us to do.

By the year 2020, they'd like fewer of us to be obese and more of us to be at a healthy weight. They'd like fewer of us to have type 2 diabetes. They'd like fewer to be suffering from osteoporosis (which means we need more calcium and vitamin D). And they'd like us to eat at least five servings a day of fruits and vegetables and at least six servings a day of whole grains, while cutting back on refined sugar and saturated fats.

How are you doing?

And here are two initiatives specifically directed at schools: They want the meals and snacks served or available at schools to have greater nutritional quality. And they want to increase the percentage of schools that teach essential nutrition topics in their classrooms.

How is your school doing?

spending more than $110 billion every year on fast food and are guzzling fifty-six *gallons* of soda per person - a whopping *six hundred* twelve-ounce cans per person per year.

Junk food and fast food aren't the only problems. Our portions have become gargantuan, whether it's at home, at the movie concession areas, or at restaurants. The huge plates coming out of the kitchen in most family restaurants are heaped with 2,000 calories or more - exceeding the total you should eat in an entire day.

And that's not all. It's the *kind* of food we eat, not just the *amount*. Remember those "food pyramids" the government has been publishing for decades now? Seems like many Americans have simply blown off those recommendations. They advise two to five cups of fruits and vegetables every day, but 42 percent of us eat only about one (and some get scarcely any). They advise that we cut back on refined grains and sugars in favor of whole grains; instead, refined sugars are often our number-one source of calories. And we eat far too much meat, eggs, high-fat dairy products, saturated fats, and salt. To top it off, the typical American gets far too little dietary fiber, a nutrient essential for heart health and cancer prevention.

Put it all together, and you get things like hamburgers, pizza, French fries, mayonnaise, butter, rich sauces, gravy, fried chicken . . . the list goes on. Sounding familiar? It's a recipe for disaster: the way most of us eat puts us at significantly increased risk of chronic illnesses, including heart disease, cancer, and type 2 diabetes.

Now throw in the mixed messages the media delivers, especially to tweens and teens. On the one hand, they are bombarded with mouth-watering ads for all kinds of fast food. On the other, they are shown that the "ideal" is the obsessively thin model. The result? An estimated 10 million girls and women and 1 million boys and men have developed eating disorders, threatening their health and well-being.

Pretty grim, isn't it? But it doesn't have to be that way. It's never too late to gradually change your habits and start making healthier choices.

What Makes Up a "Balanced" Diet

It would take a book a *lot* bigger than this one to analyze every nutrient - but it's totally possible to help you understand what's meant by a "balanced" diet in just a handful of paragraphs. Once you understand that, you can take it from there, designing an eating plan that is just right for you.

Generally, aim for a diet low in fat (especially saturated fats) and cholesterol; moderate in sugar, salt, and sodium; and rich in fruits, vegetables, whole grains, and various sources of protein. That's not as rigid as it may seem at first glance - notice that you need only *moderate* sugar, not cut it out completely. Just a few small changes can likely make a big difference in what you're feeding your body.

To eat a balanced diet that will give your body the fuel it needs to keep functioning at its best, remember four simple things:

Control your calories.
That's actually quite a personal thing that depends on how many calories you burn. Put in more calories than you burn on a regular basis, and the excess is deposited as fat. If you'd like to eat a few more calories, step up your exercise and activity level.

Get the quantity you need.
Your body needs certain quantities of vitamins, minerals, and other nutrients. Scientists have established "recommended daily allowances" that help determine how much of each you need to maintain optimum health. Labels are a good source of information about how much a product provides.

Keep things balanced.
Good health requires about forty different nutrients. Don't turn to a bottle of supplements to get them; instead, eat a healthy variety of foods.

Practice moderation.
Sure, you can eat *some* refined sugar, but remember moderation. It's okay to have a chocolate chip cookie to polish off your lunch; it's *not* okay to have a dozen.

Eat Less

Carbonated drinks

Refined sugar

Artificial sweeteners and colors

Processed foods

As you design an eating plan, take those four things into account - but make sure you're using credible, legitimate sources in the process. A simple Internet search can hook you up with more information than you'll ever need from reliable resources like the American Dietetic Association, the U.S. Food and Drug Administration, the U.S. Department of Agriculture, the American Diabetes Association, the American Cancer Society, and the American Heart Association. You can also consult your physician or a dietician or nutritionist for guidelines tailored especially to you.

An important point to remember: as you age, your nutritional needs change because your body's ability to absorb certain nutrients decreases as you get older. Those over the age of fifty need increased amounts of vitamin K, vitamin E, folic acid, niacin, riboflavin, vitamin B6, and vitamin B12, among others. You also require fewer calories as you age. It's a good idea to discuss your changing nutritional needs with your physician during your annual checkup.

How Your Diet Impacts Your Mind and Body
Now that you know the basics about nutrition, let's take a look at how it all impacts your mind and your body. Again, it would take volumes to cover it all, but here are the most important things you should know:

- Too much sugar not only causes the obvious - obesity and dental cavities - but it is also strongly related to diseases like cardiovascular disease, high blood pressure, diabetes, and even some kinds of cancers. It also leads to insulin resistance, an inability of the body to absorb available insulin, which also leads to obesity.
- Too many fats, especially saturated fats (from animal sources), lead to heart disease and certain kinds of cancers.
- Too much sodium (salt) dramatically increases the risk of high blood pressure, heart disease, and kidney disease.

A healthy diet and regular exercise have a positive effect on the general health of people with diseases or chronic conditions, and can lessen the severity of emotional disorders by giving the person a sense of greater control.

Physical fitness is not only one of the most important keys to a healthy body, it is the basis of dynamic and creative intellectual activity.

John F. Kennedy

- While alcohol isn't really a *food*, its importance can't be overlooked. It's high in calories and completely empty when it comes to nutrients. Too much of it leads to the diseases associated with inadequate nutrition and can cause liver disease; if you drink, do so in moderation.
- Getting too few essential nutrients (especially protein) can result in a poor ability to resist disease and infection, can cause deficiency diseases (such as scurvy), and can increase the risk of certain kinds of cancer. If you're pregnant, the results can be devastating - too few essential nutrients during pregnancy can result in certain birth defects, low birth weight, growth deficiencies, and some kinds of mental retardation.
- Too little calcium can cause loss of bone tissue and can lead to high blood pressure and colon cancer.
- Too little fiber in the diet increases your risk of colon cancer, certain other cancers, and a range of digestive diseases (including diverticulitis).
- Too little iron causes iron-deficiency anemia.

You've probably already heard a lot of that - but something that isn't as commonly discussed is the impact of nutrition on the brain. Your brain makes up only about 2 percent of your body's weight, but it accounts for about 25 percent of your body's metabolic demands. What that means is that if the brain is to function correctly, it needs adequate amounts of certain nutrients - including essential fatty acids, amino acids, complex carbohydrates, vitamins, minerals, and water. Now consider this: those are the same nutrients that have been shown to improve mood. The link is far from coincidental. Serious nutritional imbalances - many of which can be improved by better nutrition - exist in most people who suffer from mental disorders.

As you already know by now, the brain is filled with billions of nerve cells that enable it to communicate not only with itself but with the rest of the body. The health of those nerve cells depends on a variety of nutrients, particularly essential fatty acids - nutrients the body needs but cannot produce on its own. You need to supply those through the foods you eat, such as plant oils (including corn, safflower, canola, sesame, and soybean), green leafy vegetables, grains, nuts and seeds (especially walnuts), and cold-water fish (such as tuna, salmon, lake trout, sardines, anchovies, and mackerel). There is a strong link between inadequate essential fatty acids and depression.

A variety of nutrients have been shown to be beneficial in the treatment of depression. Other mental illnesses that have been strongly linked to inadequate nutrients include schizophrenia, bipolar disorder, anxiety, and obsessive-compulsive disorder. While nutrition is rarely the only factor in such diseases, it can be key in a treatment plan and can result in sometimes dramatic improvement.

And here's something that's discussed even less than the impact of nutrition on the brain. New research shows that the gastrointestinal tract - the first thing that receives the food you eat - actually functions like a "second brain." In fact, 95 percent of the body's serotonin and other neurotransmitters are found in the gastrointestinal tract, *not in the brain*. And that's not all; 60 percent of the immune system cells are found in the GI tract, too. Here's what that means: not only does it further prove that the mind and body are clearly related, but you have more reasons than ever to feed your body - including your GI tract - the kinds of foods that will help it stay healthy and functioning as it should.

We've just scratched the surface concerning the myriad of nutrients you need in order to do that, but with the basics you have, you can get the rest online with a few simple clicks of the mouse. Go out and learn as much as you need, then set a plan that's just right for you. As one nutritionist said, "A truly solid plan involves, well, . . . planning. So many people miss this part, but it's not that hard. Take a realistic look at where you are today, and make an aggressive, but realistic plan for change. Instead of having goals, have a vision and see yourself succeeding several times per day."

The Positive Effects of Aerobic Exercise

You've probably been hearing it all your life, but we're going to say it one more time: healthy eating is only one part of the equation when it comes to maintaining physical well-being. The other major component is exercise. And if you're lucky enough to already be at an ideal weight, don't even think about skipping this section. Weight loss is *not* the only reason you need exercise: exercise not only burns excess calories and helps create a positive energy balance, but it plays a powerful role in the other complex factors related to nutrition and provides a host of other benefits to the mind, body, and spirit.

Simply stated, you need to get moving. When it comes to exercise, frequency and regularity are more important than intensity. You're better off to do some kind of aerobic exercise fifteen or twenty minutes a day, five days a week, than to head to the gym for a grueling two-hour workout once a week.

What *is* aerobic exercise, anyway? Some people call it "cardio." It's the kind of exercise that gets your muscles moving and boosts your oxygen intake, working your heart and lungs along with your arms and legs. It's *not* strength (or resistance) training, though it does improve your overall strength and flexibility.

Exercise improves your sleep. Poor sleep is not an inevitable consequence of aging and quality sleep is important for your overall health. Exercise often improves sleep, helping you fall asleep more quickly and sleep more deeply.

Exercise boosts mood and self-confidence. Endorphins produced by exercise can actually help you feel better. Being active and feeling strong naturally helps you feel more self-confident.

Exercise is good for your brain. Exercise benefits regular brain functions and can help keep the brain active.

My grandmother started walking five miles a day when she was sixty. She's ninety-seven now, and we don't know where the heck she is.

Ellen DeGeneres

Exercise Daily: Physical, Emotional, Mental, Social, Spiritual Benefits

Keeps muscles strong and body toned

Helps maintain ideal body weight

Is a natural antidepressant

Keeps you from doing less healthy things

Helps maintain cognitive function

Prevents/helps disease

Social interaction with healthy individuals

Feel naturally high

Serve as a meditative and spiritual function

Moving is part of nature.

There are so many options when it comes to aerobic exercise that you never need to get bored, and you can find activities that fit the bill whether you want to exercise indoors, outdoors, or both. Some good examples of aerobic exercise include stair climbing, spinning (using a stationary bicycle), walking, running, inline skating, cross-country skiing, rowing, circuit training, swimming laps, kickboxing, gardening, jumping rope, and water aerobics - and that's just to name a few. You can also join a group or class, such as Zumba or other types of aerobics.

One of the best aerobic exercises you can do is also one of the most simple: go for a brisk walk! You don't need any complicated or expensive equipment, you can do it almost anywhere, and it doesn't require any fancy training. Walking has gained accolades not only from the medical profession but from people in all walks of life. Philosopher and author Henry David Thoreau claimed, "An early-morning walk is a blessing for the whole day." German philosopher and cultural critic Friedrich Nietzsche maintained that "all truly great thoughts are conceived while walking." And the brilliant ancient Greek physician Hippocrates alluded to the power of exercise on the mind when he wrote, "If you are in a bad mood, go for a walk. If you are still in a bad mood, go for another walk." And let's not forget Thomas Jefferson's advice when it came to exercise: "Walking is the best possible exercise. Habituate yourself to walk very far."

So remember that "regular aerobic exercise" can consist of something as simple and enjoyable as a daily walk; you might follow up a simple lunch with a few laps around the school on your lunch hour if you find it difficult to carve out time for exercise. But don't be afraid to include a variety of other exercises too; mix it up and have fun with it! Just keep it up if you want to enjoy all the benefits exercise holds for you. The key is to get your heart rate up and sweat for just ten to fifteen minutes at a time.

How Exercise Affects Your Mind

Let's switch it up this time and start with the way regular aerobic exercise affects your mind. Exercise has been shown to promote positive mental health. According to the U.S. Surgeon General, exercise improves mood, reduces anxiety, improves self-esteem, and has a significant role in easing the symptoms of depression.

Researchers studying the effects of exercise on adolescents found that those who were physically inactive were more likely to suffer from depression and anxiety; they were also more likely to internalize their problems, leading to aggression. Those who got regular exercise were at significantly lower risk for mental health problems.

A significant reason why is the fact that aerobic exercise causes the brain to release endorphins, powerful chemicals that act as natural painkillers; some believe that they are more powerful than narcotic drugs. But that's not all the endorphins do: responsible for the well-known "runner's high" that accompanies exercise, they also produce a sense of calm, happiness, and well-being.

In fact, endorphins play a much more complex role than originally thought. According to *Psychology Today*, when you participate in regular aerobic exercise, the endorphins your brain pumps into your bloodstream play a role in what you feel in response to "crying, laughing, thrills from music, acupuncture, placebos, stress, depression, chili peppers, compulsive gambling, aerobics, trauma, masochism, massage, labor and delivery, appetite, immunity, near-death experiences, and playing with pets." Okay, no one wants compulsive gambling or masochism, but you get the picture. Much of what goes on in your mind and body in response to such highly emotive incidents can be traced directly to endorphins - which are released in what seems like gallons when you exercise.

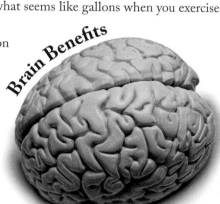

Brain Benefits

Increases production of neurochemicals that promote brain cell repair.

Prompts growth of new nerve cells and blood vessels

Improves memory

Lengthen attention span

Improves multi-tasking and planning

Boosts decision-making skills

New studies show that exercise can also boost your brainpower. In an article published in the *Washington Post*, scientists have shown that exercise has a long-term influence on a wide range of cognitive abilities and even seems to stimulate the growth of new neurons in the brain. In the study, previously sedentary adults who took up aerobic exercise improved their performance in cognitive drills after just six months of starting the exercise. That impact may be even more important as we age: studies show that those who rarely exercise are twice as likely to suffer from cognitive impairment as they get older. In those studies, older people got tremendous benefit from something as simple as cycling, gardening, or swimming just twice a week. Yet only about 10 percent of Americans over the age of sixty-five get regular exercise.

The Physical Effects of Exercise
What about the physical effects of exercise on your body?

One of the greatest benefits of exercise is that it moderates the stress response. We know that stress batters the body, knocks out immunity, and causes all kinds of problems related to the stress response. Exercise moderates and reduces stress, leading to a state of relaxation, reducing tension, and preventing stress-related diseases and illness. In fact, more than one-third of all Americans who engage in regular exercise say they do it to get rid of stress; even more do it because it helps them relax.

The physical benefits of exercise are almost too numerous to list - but take a look at some of the most important. Exercise also has a positive effect on type 2 diabetes; it's one of the best ways to control blood sugar, reduce insulin resistance, and manage diabetes. It also helps prevent type 2 diabetes. Aerobic exercise improves the heart muscle itself as well as the health of the entire cardiovascular system, reducing the risk of all kinds of heart disease. It lowers blood pressure. Regular aerobic exercise strengthens bones and prevents bone loss, dramatically reducing the risk of osteoporosis. It helps prevent cancer, particularly cancers of the breast, colon, and prostate. It also improves the health of cancer survivors and may reduce the risk of further cancer. It tones and strengthens the muscles. It helps prevent pulmonary disease by strengthening the lungs. And, while it seems counterintuitive, it reduces fatigue and improves the quality of sleep.

Finally, regular aerobic exercise helps you live longer!

Exercise Benefits

Reduces body fat
Increases lifespan
Oxygenates body
Strengthen muscles
Manages chronic pain
Wards off viruses
Reduces diabetes risk
Strengthens heart
Clears arteries
Boosts mood
Maintains mobility
Improves memory
Improves coordination
Strengthens bones
Improves complexion
Detoxifies body
Decreases stress
Boosts immune system
Lowers blood pressure
Reduces cancer risk

Beginning an Exercise Program

Start out slowly

Vary your workout

Make it fun

Include others

Keep accountable

Set attainable goals

Set aside specific time

Reward yourself

Focus on long-term and not on occasional setbacks

Exercise should be regarded as tribute to the heart.

Gene Tunney

Important Tips to Remember

Convinced? As you start out on your improved exercise program, there are a few tips you should remember. First, no matter your age, the most beneficial exercise for you is what we call "mind-body exercise" - activities that combine body movement with controlled breathing and mental focus. These kinds of activities help unite your mind, body, and spirit, giving you the greatest possible benefits from your exercise.

Other tips to remember include these:

- If you're new to an exercise program, start slow. As one exercise physiologist put it, "Exercise to stimulate, not to annihilate. The world wasn't formed in a day, and neither were we." Set small goals and build on them.
- Choose activities you enjoy; your exercise should be something to which you look forward and in which you will regularly participate.
- Include variety by doing a number of different activities. If you get bored, it's tough to keep up your motivation to exercise.
- If you're having a hard time keeping up your motivation, consider finding a partner who will exercise with you. Not only will it be more enjoyable, but you'll be accountable to each other for following through.
- Warm up by doing gentle stretches before you start exercising, even if you're doing something as simple as walking. Remember to stretch the muscles of your chest as well as your limbs; your chest will be working harder to move air. Accomplished Olympic runner and three-time gold medalist Florence Griffith Joyner advised, "A muscle is like a car. If you want it to run well early in the morning, you have to warm it up."
- Make sure to breathe deeply and regularly while you exercise. You're working out your heart, lungs, and muscles, and they need increased oxygen. Relax your breathing by rolling your shoulder muscles up and back, then relaxing.
- Guard against dehydration by drinking four to eight ounces of water every twenty minutes to replace the water you lose in sweat. If you feel thirsty while exercising, you're already dehydrated; stop immediately and drink some water before continuing your session.
- Literally ground yourself by planting your bare feet on the earth either before or after exercising.
- Consider yoga; it's good for the mind, spirit, and body.
- Listen to your body; if you feel pain while doing a certain activity, stop. If the pain lasts for more than a few days, see your doctor.
- Cool down when you finish exercising by doing more gentle stretches. Your goal is to relax the muscles, lower your heart rate, and help your body recover from the stress of the workout.
- Don't overdo it; you'll injure your muscles. You should rest your muscles for twenty-four hours between each exercise session.
- Above all, have fun! This isn't a temporary thing you're doing to lose weight or train for a 5K. Regular exercise, just like healthy eating, needs to be a permanent part of your life that will build wellness.

The Third Leg of the Stool: Quality, Adequate Sleep

You've now got the basics of nutrition and exercise under your belt. Time to attend to the third essential for good health: an adequate amount of quality sleep each night. Sleep is what regenerates your body after a long day dealing with all kinds of demands, and it's essential for wellness.

If you're like most Americans, you don't get enough sleep. Various studies have come up with slightly different numbers, but the general consensus is that we don't get enough sleep - and what we do get tends to be bothersome or less restful that it needs to be. As many as half of all Americans complain to their doctors about not getting enough sleep; in fact, it's the third most common symptom mentioned to doctors. Fatigue (which can be a natural byproduct of sleep deprivation) is number one.

That lack of quality sleep affects everything we do. In one comprehensive survey, half of all Americans said that on at least one day a week, they were too tired during their waking hours to do the things expected of them. Almost a fifth of those polled said they felt that way *every single* day.

How much sleep do you need? Sleep needs vary from person to person. Most people need seven to eight hours of sleep each night in order to feel good throughout the next day. Extremes vary from less than six hours to ten or more hours, though those are uncommon. How do you know what your own personal requirement is? You need enough to feel energized, fully restored, and alert throughout the next day. If you find yourself nodding off, feeling "bushed," unable to focus, or physically dragging during the day, you probably need more sleep.

As a nation, we're getting far less sleep than our grandparents and great-grandparents did, and there are lots of reasons why. For one thing, before the widespread acceptance and use of electric lighting, people simply went to sleep when it got dark. Today, we can - and do - stay up until all hours of the night. Then consider the lure of television and electronics; many Americans have televisions in their bedroom, and plenty are propped up against the pillows with a laptop or iPad. And consider the type of work we do: fifty to seventy-five years ago, most people were farmers, laborers, or factory workers - the type of work you couldn't bring home. Today, most of us can bring our work home with us, and it's tough to pull the plug at night when there's still so much to do. And then there are the workaholics who have convinced themselves that sleep is a waste of time they could be spending on something much more important. As a final factor, many Americans now take medications that hadn't even been formulated in our parents' day - medications that often interfere with sleep.

And those are just the run-of-the-mill, everyday reasons why so many of us battle with sleep. For some, sleep problems fall into the category of *insomnia*, a long-term or chronic inability to get enough sleep. There are several different kinds of insomnia:

- You have trouble *falling* asleep when you go to bed; you seem to toss and turn forever before finally going to sleep. This kind of insomnia may be caused by anxiety, but it can also be caused by a poor "sleep environment" - your room is too hot, too cold, too noisy, or not dark enough. This kind of insomnia can also occur if your body temperature is too high.
- You have trouble *staying* asleep. You might wake up multiple times during the night or might wake up too early in the morning (without getting enough sleep). A few factors commonly cause people to wake up too early - that often happens if you are depressed or need to use the bathroom, and is much more common as we age (and require less sleep). Waking up often during the night can also be caused by

Sleep is that golden chain that ties health and our bodies together.

Thomas Dekker

Think in the morning. Act in the noon. Eat in the evening. Sleep in the night.

William Blake

depression, needing to use the bathroom, or a medical concern, such as acid reflux, obstructive sleep apnea (especially when accompanied by loud snoring), or heart failure. Waking up numerous times during the night is not necessarily a problem unless it is difficult for you to quickly fall back to sleep.

- You *perceive* that you're not getting enough sleep. No matter how much sleep you get, you don't feel refreshed the next day.

An especially troublesome symptom of insomnia is daytime sleepiness, generally resulting from either too little sleep or sleep that is not deeply restful and refreshing. This can be caused by medical problems (such as the ones already listed), but it can also be caused by trying to subterfuge your natural sleep cycle. That's especially common in teens, and you might have noticed it in your students. Everybody has an "internal clock" that tells them when it's time to go to bed and time to wake up. When you deliberately ignore that internal clock - staying up until 2 a.m. and sleeping until 10 a.m., for example - you can develop what's called "sleep phase delay." Your internal clock gets messed up, your body gets confused, and no one knows when bedtime really is.

Why Sleep Is Important

Sleep Cycles

Sleeping pills help you fall asleep, but will not help you get to Stage 5.

Stage 1
Interim between consciousness and sleep. Light sleep. Muscle activity slows down. Occasional muscle twitching.

Stage 2
Breathing pattern and heart rate slows. Slight decrease in body temperature. Brain does less complicated tasks.

Stage 3
Deep sleep begins. Brain begins to generate slow delta waves. Body makes repairs.

Stage 4
Very deep sleep. Rhythmic breathing. Limited muscle activity. Brain produces delta waves. Body temperature and blood pressure decrease.

Stage 5
Light Rapid eye movement. Brainwaves speed up and dreaming occurs. Muscles relax and heart rate increases. Breathing is rapid and shallow.

So what's the big deal about sleep? Research has shown that there are three major reasons why it's critical to get enough sleep:

Repair. Here's a seemingly little-known fact: your body does almost all of its healing while you sleep. That's because most of our growth hormone is secreted as we sleep. You may be thinking that you're way past the time when you need any growth hormone, but you would be mistaken. Every day, during normal activities, we all sustain "micro-injuries" throughout our bodies - the microscopic tears in muscle and other tissue that occur as a result of normal wear and tear. That growth hormone you're pumping out during the deep stages of sleep? That's what fixes all of those injuries, making you good as new by morning. It's not difficult to figure out that if those micro-injuries aren't fixed day after day, you're soon feeling really bad.

And ever noticed that when you get a cold or the flu, all you want to do is sleep? That's your body's way of telling you that you *need* to go to sleep so it can go to work making you better.

Restoration. Your nervous system is a vast and complex network of neurotransmitters, the cells that do all the critical communication throughout the body. After a long, hard day, they need to be restored and refreshed, and that's what happens when you sleep. During sleep your brain is also busy, putting out chemicals like serotonin, dopamine, and norepinephrine, all of which relieve pain, depression, and anxiety. After a good night's sleep, you wake up feeling restored, because you are. Mess with that, and you wake up depressed, anxious, and hurting.

Integration. Here's a less-known fact about sleep: While you drift away in the deep stages of sleep, your mind is working overtime, organizing new memory and putting all the experiences you had during the day into some kind of world view. Good, deep sleep is essential to your mental well-being. In fact, a deprivation of deep sleep can cause psychotic symptoms to develop.

Everyone has a night here or there when for one reason or another, he or she doesn't get enough quality sleep. The problem comes when that happens a lot or becomes chronic. Take a look at some of the problems associated with a long-term lack of quality sleep:

- An increased risk of depression - and that works both ways. An estimated 90 percent of all people with depression have insomnia, and people with insomnia are thirty-five times more likely to develop depression.
- Accidents. People with insomnia have four times as many car accidents as people who sleep well - a rate comparable to driving under the influence of alcohol. And the accidents aren't limited to the highways; sleep-deprived people have all kinds of other accidents. Some of the well-known accidents caused by human error due to sleepy workers include the disastrous launch of the Space Shuttle Challenger in 1986, the nuclear disasters at Three Mile Island and Chernobyl, and the massive oil spill from the Exxon Valdez tanker.
- Alcoholism. People with sleep problems are 2.4 times more likely to become alcoholic (which, of course, increases the risk of accidents all by itself).
- Metabolic problems. This one's a real domino effect: sleep deprivation causes malnutrition and weight changes. Those lead to increased stress hormones, which leads to insulin resistance, which leads to obesity. And consider this: children between the ages of six months and two years who get less than twelve hours of sleep a day are twice as likely to be obese by the time they turn three.
- Pain. The less sleep you get, the more pain you experience. And that can happen relatively quickly - people who are deprived of enough quality sleep for as few as two or three nights in a row can develop the same kind of pain as those suffering from fibromyalgia.
- Immune system malfunction. Deprive your body of sleep, and your immune system stops working the way it should. The result? You become much more susceptible to bacteria, viruses, illnesses, disease, and infection. Not only that, but your body loses some of its ability to heal once you do get sick.
- Hormone changes. Chronic sleep deprivation causes changes in the essential hormones your body needs. Sex hormones are dramatically reduced, as are the growth hormones, which are critical to the body's ability to heal and repair tissues.

Effects of Sleep Deprivation

Cognitive impairment

Memory lapses or loss

Irritability

Impaired moral judgement

Severe yawning

Hallucinations

Symptoms similar to ADHD

Impaired immune system

Risk of diabetes Type 2

Increase heart rate variability

Risk of heart disease

Decreased reaction time and accuracy

Tremors

Aches

Growth suppression

Risk of obesity

- Nervous system changes. Chronic sleep deprivation also causes all kinds of problems for the nervous system - things that range from seizures and tremors to an increased gag reflex and deep tendon reflexes. In addition, lack of sleep impacts the neurotransmitters in the brain, dramatically increasing the risk of depression.

How to Improve Your Sleep

If you're suffering from chronic or long-term insomnia - defined as sleep problems that have lasted longer than three weeks - it's a good idea to check with your doctor. He or she can assess the various factors that may be causing your insomnia and can design a treatment plan to help address the causes.

If, on the other hand, you're one of millions of Americans who occasionally struggle from insomnia, or if you just want to improve the quality of your sleep, try these strategies:

- Try to go to bed at the same time every night and wake up at the same time every morning; use an alarm so you will wake up at the same time, no matter how much sleep you got. This helps establish your internal sleep clock.
- Address any issues or stresses that are making you anxious before you go to bed. It's a good idea to formulate a plan to deal with them, and write down what you will do the next day. With a plan in mind, put them out of your mind when you go to bed.
- Develop a relaxing ritual that you do each night before going to bed to calm your mind, body, and soul. You might read for half an hour, soak in a warm bath, or listen to calming music. As your body and mind learn to anticipate your ritual, it's a signal that it's time to shut down and sleep.
- Don't drink any caffeine after 2 p.m. or any alcohol after dinner.
- Don't exercise within four hours of bedtime. Exercise raises your body temperature, which makes it difficult to fall to sleep. Your body needs four hours after exercise in which to cool down sufficiently for sleep.
- Nap only for 20 to 30 minutes to avoid grogginess and disruption of night sleep.
- Pay attention to your sleep environment. Your bedroom should be the right temperature, you should have the right amount of blankets so you are comfortable, the room should be dark, and there should be no or minimal noise. Your nightclothes and sheets should not be binding. Your mattress and pillow should be comfortable, neither too firm nor too soft. All of these are personal to you; make sure you are completely relaxed and comfortable.
- Once you are in bed, breathe slowly and deeply to help relax your mind and body.
- Avoid using your bed for anything other than sleeping, relaxing, or having sex. Don't catch up on work, study, watch television, answer email, read, or eat in bed; you need to establish with your mind and body that once you are in bed, it's time for sleep.
- If you can't fall asleep within ten or fifteen minutes of getting in bed, get up, leave the bedroom, and read or listen to music somewhere else in the house until you feel drowsy. Then go back to bed.
- As soon as you wake up, expose yourself to plenty of bright light, a signal to your brain that it's time to be awake.

Benefits of a Good Night's Sleep

Keeps your heart healthy

May prevent cancer

Reduces stress

Reduces inflammation

Make you more alert

Bolsters your memory

May help you lose weight

Naps make you smarter

May reduce your risk for depression

Helps the body make repairs.

Chapter 8

Experience High-Level Health and Wellness through a Mind-Body-Spirit Approach

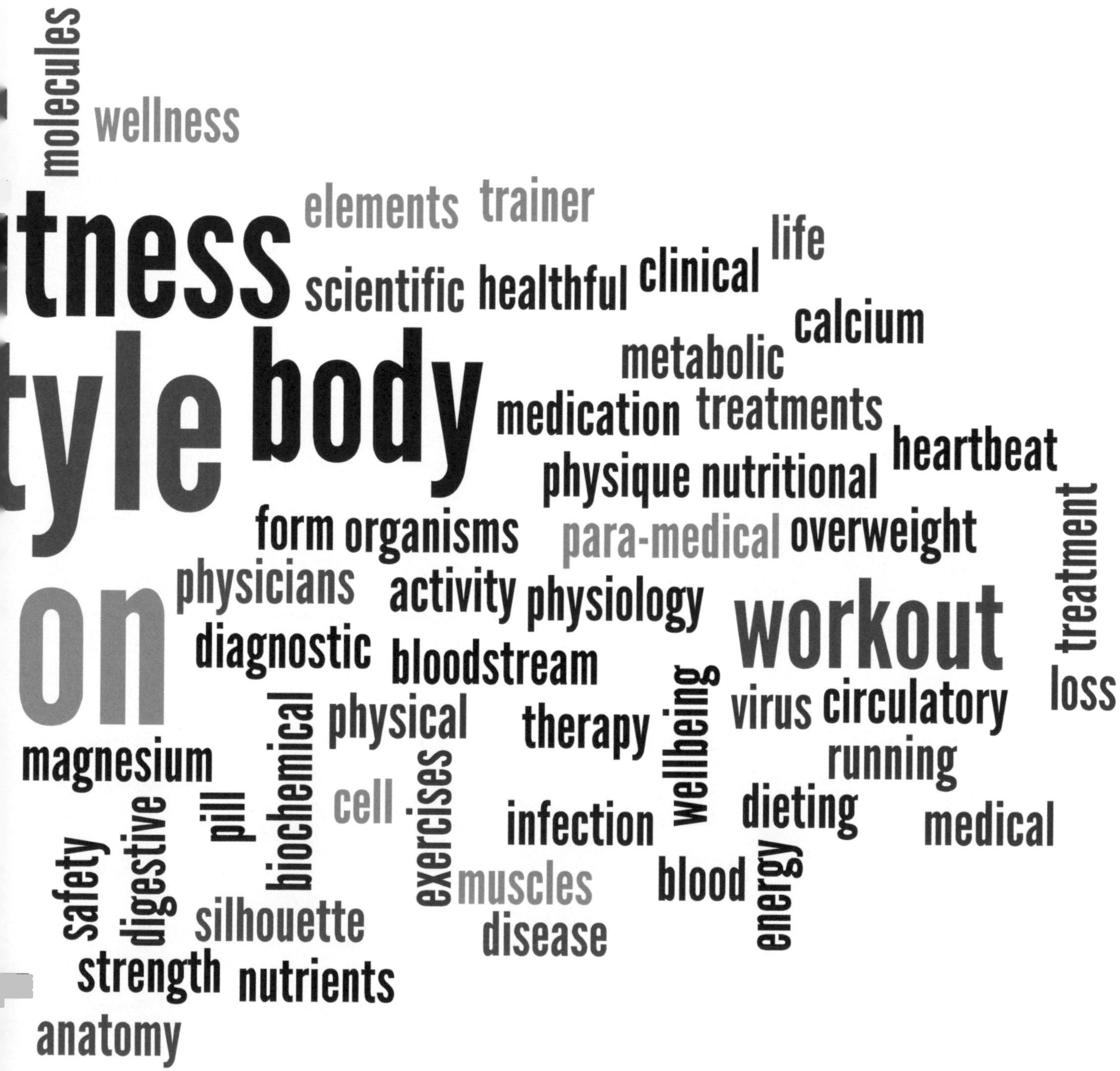

molecules

wellness

elements trainer

tness

scientific healthful clinical life

calcium

tyle body

metabolic

medication treatments

physique nutritional heartbeat

form organisms para-medical overweight

physicians activity physiology

on diagnostic bloodstream workout treatment

physical therapy virus circulatory loss

magnesium wellbeing running

cell exercises infection dieting medical

safety digestive pill biochemical blood energy

silhouette muscles

strength nutrients disease

anatomy

Chapter 8
Experiencing High-Level Health and Wellness through a Mind-Body-Spirit Approach

Bad things do happen; how I respond to them
defines my character and the quality of my life.
I can choose to sit in perpetual sadness,
immobilized by the gravity of my loss,
or I can choose to rise from the pain
and treasure the most precious gift I have –
life itself.
Walter Anderson

A well-known saying whose author is unknown points out that "the only difference between a diamond and a lump of coal is that the diamond had a little more pressure put on it."

If you're like everyone else on the planet, you're familiar with pressure, or what we commonly call *stress*. Because, after all, life is stress - in fact, life exposes us to one stressor after another. Lots of people know stress. But relatively few people on the planet have mastered the fine art of *resilience*. Webster's defines it as "the power of ability to return to the original form" or position "after being bent, compressed, or stretched." When it comes to you, *resilience* is the ability to recover readily from stress, adversity, depression, illness, and the like - a sort of buoyancy. And if there's anything that underscores the connection between mind, body, and spirit, it's resilience.

All the research points to this: resilience to stress is one of the most powerful keys to wellness. And if you want to develop that resilience, it's critical that you address the mind, body, and spirit as a whole. In this concluding chapter, we're going to give you some great suggestions on how to do exactly that.

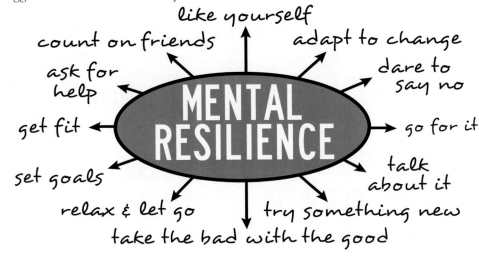

Key to Wellness: Stress Resilience

Chapter 2 introduced you to the concept of resilience; this might be a good time to review what you learned there. Because it's such an important part of wellness, we're going to give you some additional information now - information that will help you take your resilience to a whole new level.

To start, let's expand the definition of *stress resilience* a little so you can see exactly what we're talking about. For starters, people who are resilient to stress have found a way to see their stress as meaningful (which, when it comes right down to it, is closely related to finding life itself meaningful). You know the ones - and maybe you're one yourself: they see stress as an opportunity to grow and a catalyst for change. They actually *appreciate* stress and its challenges as a way to become stronger.

That's a good way to look at stress - because face it: as we pointed out before, you're going to experience stress. Betty Smith, the author of *A Tree Grows in Brooklyn*, wrote, "Everything struggles to live. Look at that tree growing up there out of that grating. It gets no sun, and water only when it rains. It's growing out of sour earth. And it's strong because its hard struggle to live is making it strong." It's like the meme that's been floating around Facebook for years: "If what doesn't kill you makes you stronger, I should be able to bench-press a Buick."

We'd like to add to that. As Derek Hough put it, "What doesn't kill you makes you a better human being. It opens your eyes, your heart, and your mind."

We've talked about the fact that stress isn't the important thing - the important thing, and the determining factor in all of it, is *how you respond to the stress*. If you become immobilized or victimized or defeated, you're facing one set of consequences. And it's not a lovely sight. But if you manage to face stress in a healthy and positive way, you come out of it wiser, stronger, and more resilient. Consider this: the Chinese pictogram for *crisis* (the very epitome of stress) combines those for *danger* and *opportunity*.

What Determines Whether Stress Is Productive or Destructive?

You might think that the severity of the stress itself determines whether it will be productive or destructive. After all, losing your job or your spouse or a child has to deal a much more calamitous blow than getting a flat tire on the way to work or dealing with frozen pipes on the weekend. Of course. No one could argue otherwise.

But here's the great part: the severity of the stress isn't what determines if it's productive or destructive. Simply, *you* determine that.

You can do three simple things to increase the chances that any stress you experience will be productive:

- Learn to see stress as an opportunity rather than a burden. You might have to do some homework to accomplish this one: your ability to see stress as an opportunity has a lot to do with whether you are an optimist in general. Those who see the world in pessimistic terms are likely to have a struggle with developing a cheerful outlook on stress.
- Go to work to see both the pros and cons of any situation and to follow through with a solution to solve the problem. Here's where a mind-body approach is especially

important: in order to sort out pros and cons and come up with solutions, you need a healthy brain - and a healthy brain depends in part on nutrition and other things you do to nourish the body. When the neurochemicals in the brain are out of whack, you have problems seeing the pros, because the pleasure center in the brain doesn't function like it should. Everything starts looking negative, and it's difficult to sort out possible solutions.

- Use tools and principles for dealing well with stress (we're about to give you some great ones you can implement in your everyday life).

Ways to Improve Your Stress Resilience

Ready to make some changes that will help you become more resilient?

We provided some great stress-management tips in Chapter 2. You'll want to go over those again and make sure you're incorporating them in your life. Now we'd like to give you some resilience tips - new tools and principles that will build on all the mind-body-spirit principles we've discussed throughout this book. These aren't quick fixes: they are the tools you can bank on for a lifetime of increased resistance, and they build on everything we've given you so far.

We've broken these into categories so you can refer back to helpful material in the previous chapters. Whatever you do, don't try to make too many changes at once. (Talk about stress!) There are a lot of tools here, and it's up to you to decide which ones you most need to implement. You're in charge. You have the opportunity to assemble your own toolbox.

Go over these suggestions, identify one or two you want to implement, and go to work! Once you've mastered those, move on to another one or two. Before you know it, you'll have a whole new arsenal with which to fuel your resilience!

Two More Tips for Stress Management (Chapter 2)

- Enjoy the process of growth and discovery that almost always comes with stress. Instead of focusing on the negatives and all the hassles, actively try to identify what you're learning and how you can come out on the other end even better. Author Nancy Farmer put it best: "The point is never to give up, even if you're falling off a cliff. You never know what might happen on the way to the bottom."
- Learn to delegate; relinquish control over the things that simply don't matter. Why make yourself crazy trying to take care of *everything* yourself? Your thirteen-year-old really can be taught how to do her own laundry, and the other fourth-grade teachers really can all take turns preparing visual aids for the history lessons you're team-teaching.

Tools for Changing Your Perception (Chapter 3)

- Do what you can to develop a sense of personal control and empowerment. That doesn't mean you should try to control others or the environment; what you're trying to control is *your response* to whatever is going on. You can't control someone else; you *can* control yourself.
- Don't just "prepare to live" - live here and now, in the moment! Too often we decide that things will be better when we've lost weight, gotten married, gotten out of

debt . . . you know the rest. Sure, those are great goals, but don't put off happiness and a full life while you're waiting for all the "good stuff." Realize that the "good stuff" is already right in front of you!

- Get into reality. Just like all people, you have your share of hopes, wishes, and fears. You're likely to deal with other people and their perceptions. That's exactly what they are - perceptions. They're not reality. Learn to grasp what is real and what is there, then act appropriately.

- Become curious. There's so much to learn and see in this world. And you don't even have to leave your own town in order to identify things you can learn more about. So, exactly why are there bubbles in carbonated beverages? How far away are the stars you see each night, and which ones have probably already burned out? You get the picture. Curiosity brings with it energy and determination, both traits that boost stress resilience.

- Be creative (a close relative of curiosity). Learn to play a musical instrument, take a water-color class, write your personal history, or try some other creative pursuit that sounds fun and interesting. Check out community courses or specialized classes at a local college.

Tools for Addressing Your Emotions (Chapter 4)

- Nourish hope. Practice having positive, optimistic expectations; it will become a habit. Along the way, you will boost your belief that you can handle anything that comes along, which also increases your sense of empowerment. Another thing to practice is your ability to envision things before they happen - figure out what a good outcome will look like, and start doing things to make it happen.

- Kick guilt in the pants. We all have things we regret - things we could have done better, things we shouldn't have done at all . . . but guilt can be a crippler that defeats your self-esteem and self-acceptance. Analyze what's causing you guilt, and list the lessons you learned from that experience. You might even want to write down how you'll avoid making that kind of mistake again. Then put guilt away and move forward.

- Exercise gratitude. You've probably seen hundreds of beautiful sunsets in your lifetime - but look at each new one with a sense of appreciation. Never lose the ability to enjoy the things around you, and express your gratitude often, even for the little things.

- Improve your sense of humor. Practice looking for the humor in even the most seemingly dire events. One woman did an entire comedy routine for her staff as she related the experience of a crown on her front tooth falling out and clunking to the table in an important board of directors meeting. Everyone in the room was in tears from laughing so hard - and she was able to reframe what could have been a devastating embarrassment.

- Practice focusing on the here and now instead of being impatient to move on to something else. Enjoy what's happening right now.

- Make it a point to be more patient.

Tools for Improving Social Support (Chapter 5)

- Develop deep relationships with other people. That might be your spouse, your child, your parent, or a good friend. Such relationships require a lot of time and effort, but they're worth it - the sense of intimacy and support increase resilience.

- Be gentle with other people and allow them the benefit of the doubt. Accept that we all (including you) have frailties and imperfections; learn to appreciate and love the good in other people and humanity in general.
- Develop a sense of independence. While we should all be connected to others in healthy ways, you shouldn't become dependent on someone else for approval, love, respect, or destiny. Those things are all great when we receive them, but they should be *added* to what we already know for ourselves.
- Celebrate and champion the people around you. Take joy in their victories and successes. Be the one at faculty meeting who points out a really cool thing the kindergarten teacher came up with and implemented in her classroom. The only real "competition" is with yourself, not others.
- Love - love deeply and passionately. That applies not just to the important people in your life, but to yourself as well. You don't need to be arrogant or offensive about it, but become your own biggest fan. Cherish the things about you that make you *you*. Forgive yourself. Treat yourself gently and kindly. Be confident in your ability to handle whatever comes along.

Tools for Enhancing Spirituality (Chapter 6)

- Develop an appreciation for yourself: value yourself for who you are right now, not the person you hope to become later in life. Accept yourself for who you *are*, not just what you do. Realize that mistakes are an opportunity for learning and growth, not a reason to give up or collapse. And never let a mistake define you.
- Examine your deepest values, and pledge to live by those values no matter what kind of pressure you're experiencing to abandon them. Holding true to your values and being congruent in how you live will increase your sense of self-worth, which is a necessary part of resilience.
- Work on being connected - to others, to the earth, to the cosmos, and to the sources of your spiritual strength. As you increase your sense of connectedness, you will develop or increase traits like kindness, humor, forgiveness, and empathy. Most of all, be connected to your deepest self and treat yourself with the respect you deserve.

- Cultivate a sense of meaning and purpose in life. We talked about this earlier, and it's important to your resilience. Decide what's important to you and why you're here; you might go so far as to define a "mission" for your life. Doing so will help you create or strengthen a vision of your potential and will help you find wisdom and strength in any difficulties you're facing.

Today's Revolution: The Mind-Body-Spirit Approach

In the last century and a half, there have been some significant revolutions in the field of medicine. First came the advent of ether anesthesia, which kicked off a surgical revolution in the mid1800s (after all, who relishes the thought of surgery without *anesthesia*?). That was followed in about 1870 by the scientific revolution, when scientists learned to conduct tests and clearly demonstrate repeatable results - still a critical skill being used today. Then in the 1930s came a chemical revolution that began with penicillin, a drug that changed the face of medical treatment worldwide. A stroll into your local pharmacy will underscore the results.

But when it comes to medicine, those of us alive on the planet right now find ourselves in the middle of what is likely the most exciting revolution of all. In the first place, emphasis has shifted from *treating disease* to *preventing disease*. In other words, we've finally worked around to the notion that there are many things we can to do increase the odds of staying well - and staying well beats getting sick any day of the week.

The second important part of this revolution is that we are finally recognizing the critical connection between the mind, the body, and the spirit. What that means is that you're getting lots of good information about how to keep your body well - including things like good nutrition, plenty of aerobic exercise, and lots of good sleep, as we discussed in Chapter 7. But along with that, wellness experts are touting the importance of many other factors that lead to wellness - things like strong social support, good stress management, a sense of purpose, hope, effective anger control, faith, a sense of personal control, and an optimistic outlook, to name a few. And all of that is important because experts now realize that the mind, body, and spirit are inseparably connected and must function as a whole if we are to enjoy optimal health.

As we move into the future on the wave of this foremost revolution, we anticipate the time when, as French neurologist Frederic Tilney predicted, "We will by conscious command evolve cerebral centers which will permit us to use powers that we now are not even capable of imagining."

Ours is the behavioral revolution - the recognition that the way we choose to behave as we address mind, body, and spirit determines the way we will move throughout the rest of our lives in either optimal wellness or its opposite.

A Mind-Body-Spirit Model for Wellness

Before giving you the basic components of a mind-body-spirit model for wellness, let's talk a little about change. Obviously, your efforts to incorporate parts of this model into your life will require some level of change - adopting something new, replacing an old habit with a different way of doing things.

There's no question about it: change can be hard. It yanks us away from the things we know and propels us out of our comfort zones. Change can be especially hard when we are stressed: in the face of stress, your mind, body, and spirit all become overly aroused, making it extremely difficult to relax and focus on anything new.

The important first step in change, then, is eliciting the relaxation response, a term coined by a Harvard cardiologist to describe a state in which the mind, body, and spirit are tranquil, calm, and stress-free. When you prompt the relaxation response, your parasympathetic nervous system takes over and everything in your body works better, including your immune system.

There are lots of ways to get into that state, and we'll discuss some of them in a minute. For now, suffice it to say that you need to relax if you want to change!

There are four basic elements you need to employ in your effort to make any change:

- **Relax.** As we just mentioned, you need to get rid of stress in order to successfully change. We'll provide some great methods for relaxation in just a minute.

The relaxation response is a physical state of deep rest that changes the physical and emotional responses to stress — and the opposite of the fight or flight response.

Herbert Benson, M.D.
Harvard Medical School

- **Be aware.** First off, be aware of *yourself*. Understand that you are in control. Period. *You* can respond to any situation exactly the way you decide to. That's not all: become completely aware of how you do react in specific situations, especially those dealing with the things you want to change. Pretend you're studying for an important exam - analyze what you do, why you do it, what happens as a result, and how you would rather do things.

- **Design the new.** *Clearly* determine what you want the new behavior to be. And we do mean *clearly*. This will take a bit of work, but it's worth it. Be specific. Write it down. Envision yourself behaving in the new way - whether it's choosing a handful of baby carrots over a doughnut for your midmorning snack or reacting in a different way to a colleague who consistently hassles you. In writing, literally script your new behavior/response. You might feel stuck on this step - you know you want to change, but you're not sure what you want the new behavior to be. If so, think about a person you admire for some ideas you can incorporate; you might also consider your deepest wisdom, values, and ideals for ideas on how you'd like to behave.

- **Practice.** Now that you've settled on the change you'd like to make, *practice!* If it's a mental or emotional change, visualize your new response over and over; if it's a physical change, literally do it repeatedly. The more you are able to perform the changed behavior, the more quickly it will become a habit. And with that, guess what? Your new, improved, changed behavior will then be your new comfort zone!

Ready to get started? Use the following parts of the model to construct your own new reality of mind-body-spiritual wellness.

A Sense of Personal Empowerment

Ever tried to put together an intricate puzzle only to find that a couple of pieces were missing? Or how about trying to build a model airplane only to find that you have two of one part and none of another? No matter how hard you try, you can't achieve the whole, finished piece.

Well, that's how personal empowerment is when it comes to achieving complete wellness. It's at the heart of stress resilience and all its connected parts. Why? If you don't enjoy a sense of personal empowerment, you will be easily overwhelmed by any distressing situation that comes along. You'll cave in to stress. You'll be jettisoned along, thrown here and there by whatever is going on. And change? If you don't have a sense of personal empowerment, you won't even *consider* change, because you won't believe it's within your grasp.

And here's a delicious little side effect of a sense of empowerment: when you feel in control of yourself and your ability to react to the world, your brain chemistry sits up and takes notice. One of the major resulting benefits is increased production of serotonin and endorphins, the chemicals that activate the pleasure center in your brain and help to boost immunity.

So how do you gain a better sense of personal empowerment? We need to start by discussing a seeming paradox. The more you try to control your external situation - how other people act, for example - the more out of control you will feel. You simply can't reliably change anyone or anything other than yourself. You'll never be able to make your principal a more optimistic person, nor can you make your neighbor across the street move the shed that's blocking your view.

The sign of an intelligent people is the ability to control their emotions by the application of reason.

Marya Mannes

127

What should you do, then? Let go. The more you let go when it comes to controlling anything outside yourself, the greater sense of control you will feel. That's because you will be working on controlling the thing you *can* control: you and your responses!

Here are a few additional suggestions you might try:

- If you find yourself constantly trying to control other people or things, it might be a sign your brain's serotonin levels are deficient. Inspiring you to control others just might be your brain's attempt to increase its serotonin levels. Instead of being a control freak, try some better ways to increase serotonin: meditate (more about that in a minute), get plenty of restful sleep, and eat foods high in tryptophan (an amino acid that converts into serotonin). Good sources of tryptophan are cheese, including cheddar, parmesan, mozzarella, Romano, Swiss, edam, gruyere, and gouda; soybeans and soy foods, such as tofu; seeds and nuts, including sesame seeds, sunflower seeds, chia seeds, flaxseeds, cashews, almonds, pistachio nuts, and hazelnuts; red meat, chicken, and turkey; fish; oats; lentils; and eggs.
- Realize and nurture your power and ability to be the way you want to be, regardless of what's going on around you.
- Refuse to blame other people for "making" you respond in ways you don't like or don't want. No one else can make you do anything. Important to a personal sense of empowerment is accepting responsibility for yourself and the way you behave.
- One of the greatest keys for a sense of personal empowerment is to be aware of your own wisdom and integrity and to listen to them.

Cognitive Structure

Cognitive is a word that relates to the way you think, and cognitive structure is a way of changing your thinking. After all, it's not a stressful situation that controls us - instead, it's the way we think about the situation that holds all the power. Hence, cognitive structure is a way of helping you change the way you *think* and respond.

There's a three-fold sequence that rapidly occurs every time something happens in your world:

- A situation occurs.
- You think about the situation.
- You respond to your thoughts with emotions, physical reactions, and behavior.

This sequence occurs without you even having to think about it - and it happens so fast that before you know it, you're already responding.

Time to slow down!

Here's the key: *you* are the one who chooses how you will think about the situation. *You* are the one who determines what meaning it has for you. You are the one who decides how you will respond. Got that? In other words, *you* are in control - the situation has absolutely no control. If you blame your thoughts, feelings, and responses on the situation, you are giving up your control. You become a victim.

It all starts in your head and depends on what you think. Remember that you choose the way you think. If you can change your thinking, your response will also change.

Here's how it works. Let's say two teachers get called to the principal's office. The first automatically decides she's in trouble - she has clearly done something to irk the principal and is now being called in for a sound thrashing. As she steps into the hall on her way to the office, she thinks, *I hate that woman! My job would be so much easier if I didn't have to worry all the time about things like this!* By the time she gets to the office, she is grinding her teeth, her stomach is in knots, and sweat has beaded up on her forehead.

The second teacher gets the same call, but things go much differently for him. He thinks, *I know the principal is looking for some people to be on that art committee, and I'd really enjoy that. Maybe that's what she wants to talk to me about.* He is relaxed and open as he walks down the hall to the office.

What was the difference between the two teachers? It wasn't the situation - they both got the same phone call. The difference was in their thoughts, which, in turn, made the difference in how they felt and acted.

Here are a few suggestions for changing your cognitive structure:

- Try to slow down! When something starts to happen, imagine a big, bright-red stop sign. Exercise your will to avoid *automatically* reacting to the situation. Instead, pause and take a few deep breaths.
- Get calm. As long as you're upset, excited, stressed, or frightened, you won't be able to come up with a better, wiser way of handling things.
- Now that you're calm, check your thoughts. Are they rational? In the example above, why would you automatically leap to the conclusion that you were in trouble because you've been called to the principal's office? Maybe there's a large package she needs you to pick up. Maybe a concerned parent wants to talk about a child who is bullying her daughter. It could be any number of things. Focus on coming up with a more rational way of thinking about the situation.
- If you find that your thoughts are destructive or stressful, *change them.*
- Avoid blaming anyone or anything else for your thoughts or feelings. You're in charge.
- As long as you think someone else is the culprit, you give all the control to that person and you become the hapless victim.

If you find yourself in a repeated difficult situation, try the technique of visualization. In a quiet, comfortable place free from distraction, close your eyes and visualize yourself about to get into the situation. Go through the whole scenario, "practicing" how you will change your thinking and how as a result your whole reaction will change. In your mind, see how much better you feel. Do it as many times as you need to so that the next time you're in that situation, you will "automatically" choose the better way of thinking and responding.

If needed, a good cognitive therapist can help you hone this skill.

Meditation and Relaxation

You already know that staying calm and peaceful is an important part of mind-body-spirit wellness. You should also know that research has shown that various kinds of meditation and relaxation can actually help you change behaviors.

There are all kinds of books and resources for learning meditation and relaxation techniques. Besides swinging by your favorite bookstore or library, check out the Internet for instruction and information about the diverse types of meditation and relaxation that might help you. You might want to try out a few different methods before settling on one or two that provide the most benefit.

Regardless of the type of meditation or relaxation you try, there are a few basics. Find a quiet, comfortable place free of distractions where you won't be interrupted; if you have young children at home, you might want to do it before they wake up in the morning or after they go to bed at night. Make sure the temperature is at a comfortable level and that you are seated in a physically comfortable place and position. Turn off your cell phone.

Following are just a few of the different kinds of meditation and relaxation you might want to try:

Quiet contemplation.
Delve into your deepest thoughts and think about your deepest values. Consider how you would like things to be right now. Write down your thoughts, and include what you would be hearing, seeing, smelling, feeling, and sensing in that situation. Now write what having this outcome would mean to you. This sort of exercise helps motivate you to work toward change.

Progressive muscle relaxation.
For this exercise, you will start with one part of your body and then sequentially go through the rest. Here's how it works: As you breathe in, tense the muscles of your right arm, including your hand. Make a tight fist and really tense up your arm. Hold your breath for a moment and really focus on how the tenseness feels. Then, as you exhale, completely relax that same group of muscles. Let your arm drop and your hand fall into your lap. Focus on what relaxation feels like. Do the same thing with all the muscle groups in your body, from head to toe. Next time you start to feel stressed, you'll suddenly realize that your muscles are tense - and you'll know a way to relax.

Visualization.
As the name would imply, visualization enables you to focus your thoughts on a specific situation, whether real or imagined; it is an effective way of helping reframe your thoughts about and reactions to traumatic or potentially frightening situations. Imagine yourself in the situation, then imagine changing your thoughts about that situation so that it becomes less traumatic, frightening, or threatening. Finally, imagine yourself reacting in a calmer, better, and more productive way. Visualization allows you to practice "seeing" yourself feeling and acting the way you want.

Meditative breathing.
The purpose of meditative breathing is to calm both your mind and your body. This is a classic mind-body exercise that shows how related the two are (think about the last time you were in a panic, and remember how rapidly you were breathing!). To practice meditative breathing, take in a slow, deep breath until your lungs are completely full; as you do, place your hand on your abdomen, over your diaphragm, and notice how your diaphragm rises as you take in air. Hold your breath for a moment, really focusing on the feeling of fullness. Then slowly exhale, noticing how your diaphragm sinks as your lungs empty. As you continue to practice, you will feel yourself becoming increasingly more calm. Once you master this technique, you can actually calm yourself simply by placing your hand on your abdomen!

The Spiritual Connection

True well-being cannot exist in the absence of a spiritual connection, a sense that brings meaning and fulfillment to life. Healing and wellness rely on genuine spiritual growth, a sense of empowerment, connectedness, and meaning. You can realize optimum wellness when you have a purpose in life and find great meaning in the things you do and the people with whom you associate.

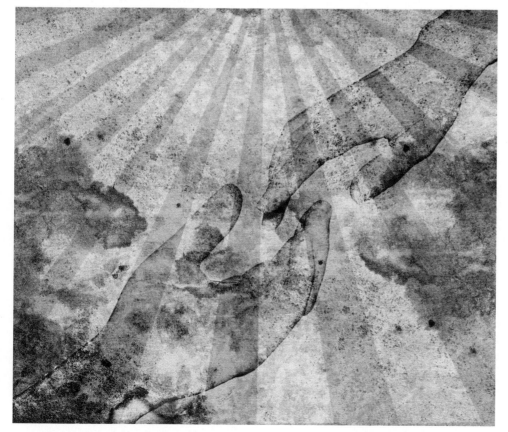

Part of spiritual wellness involves your deepest values and the things that are most important to you. When you are living in a way that respects your deepest values, you experience the kind of fulfillment that leads to true spiritual wellness. When your thoughts and behaviors betray your deepest values, you experience guilt, shame, and diminished well-being.

Chapter 6 provides detailed information about spirituality and its importance to well-being. In summary, you should strive to develop the following solid spiritual practices:

- Empower yourself to live with integrity. That means clinging to your deepest values and the things that are most important to you, regardless of what is going on around you. If you find yourself in a compromising situation, it might mean leaving that situation, even if it seems very difficult to do so.
- Do whatever you can to increase your capacity to love. Practice seeing the good in others. Serve them. Forgive them. Cherish them.
  Build your connections to the positive things in life. You should be connected to your loved ones, others, nature, the universe, and a higher power.
- Identify your purpose in life. Make sure that the things you are doing contribute to that purpose, not detract from it. If you find yourself neglecting that purpose, consider making some changes in how you're living life.
- Do something meaningful to you every day. That might be as simple as rocking a child to sleep or as monumental as working on an important project.
- Foster hope - in yourself and in others.

Now at the end, you might ask what kind of a difference all of this mind-body-spirit stuff can make. Countless researchers and scientists and experts in many fields have the answer: it can make a significant difference in how well you are, how happy your life is, and how long you live. The information we've given you throughout this book, when practiced consistently, can actually prevent or alter the course of disease. We'll give you just one example: a physician at the University of Massachusetts Medical Center Stress Reduction Clinic took on more than four thousand sick people on whom doctors had given up. The doctors were at their wits' end, and so were the patients. By doing nothing more than helping those patients learn effective stress reduction techniques, the physician "cured" the illnesses in more than a third of them. And that's just one example.

Former Egyptian president Anwar Sadat said, "He who cannot change the very fabric of his thought will never be able to change reality." In these pages, we have tried to provide the tools that will help you change the very fabric of your thought, a process that can take you on the adventure of your life - an adventure that will culminate in the reality of optimum wellness, a deep sense of joy, and a long and satisfying life.

Now, it's up to you!

The Four Core Principles of Well-Being

A feeling of personal control and empowerment.

This involves a sense of feeling valued and heard, an ability to control our responses, and the ability to live by our deepest values.

A sense of meaning and purpose.

This involves finding meaning and purpose in the present, enjoying the process of creativity and growth, having a caring sense of mission, and having a clear vision of our potential.

A sense of acceptance and connectedness.

To the sources of our spiritual strength, which involves forgiveness, humor and kindness.

To our deepest self, to other people, and to the earth and cosmos.

A feeling of hope.

This involves the ability to envision what we want to have happen in our lives, positive optimistic expectations, and the confidence that we can deal successfully with situations that come our way.

Endnotes

Chapter 1

Brad Lemley, "What Is Integrative Medicine?" DrWeil.com News, accessed from www.drweil.com/drw/u/ART02054/Andrew-Weil-Integrative-Medicine.html

D. M. Eisenberg, R. C. Kessler, C. Foster, F. E. Norlock, D. R. Calkins, and T. L. Delbanco, "Unconventional Medicine in the United States," New England Journal of Medicine, vol. 246 (1998).

Delia Rossetto Chiaramonte, "Mind-Body Therapies for Primary Care Physicians," Primary Care 24, no. 4 (December 1997): 788.

J. M. Starr, J. Wardlaw, and K. Ferguson, "Increased Blood Brain Barrier Permeability in Type II Diabetes Demonstrated by Gadolinium Magnetic Resonance Imaging," Journal of Neurology, Neurosurgery & Psychiatry 74 (2003), 70.

Joel S. Lazar, "Mind-Body Medicine in Primary Care: Implications of Applications," Primary Care 23, no. 1 (March 1996): 169.

L. D. Kubzansky et al., "Angry Breathing: A Prospective Study of Hostility and Lung Function in the Normative Aging Study," Thorax, October 2006. See also S. Cohen, D. A. Tyrell, and A. P. Smith, "Psychological Stress and Susceptibility to the Common Cold," New England Journal of Medicine 325 (1991): 606–612.

"Laughter Is the Best Medicine," Science Daily (January 26, 2008).

M. F. Scheier and C. S. Carver, "A Model of Behavioral Self-Regulation: Translating Intention into Action," pp. 303–46 in Louise Berkowitz, ed., Advances in Experimental Social Psychology, vol. 21 (New York: Academic Press, 1988).

M. Viljoen, A. Panzer, J.L. Roos, and W. Bodemer, "Psycho-neuroimmunology: From Philosophy, Intuition, and Folklore to a Recognized Science," South African Journal of Science 99 (July/August 2003): 332.

Penelope Wang, Karen Springen, Tom Schmitz, and Mary Bruno, "A Cure for Stress?" Newsweek (October 12, 1987), 84–85.

R. N. Kalaria, et al., "The -Glucose Transporter of the Human Brain and Blood Brain Barrier," Annals of Neurology 24 (1988), 757.
Redford B. Williams and Margaret A. Chesney, "Psychosocial Factors and Prognosis in Established Coronary Artery Disease," Journal of the American Medical Association 270 (1993): 1860–1861.

S. M. Samuelsson, B. Bauer Alfredson, B. Hagberg, G. Samuelsson, B. Nordbeck, A. Brun, L. Gustafson, and J.

Risberg, "The Swedish Centenarian Study: A Multidisciplinary Study of Five Consecutive Cohorts at the Age of 100," International Journal of Aging and Human Development 45 (3; 1997): 223–53.

Shakti Gawain, The Path of Transformation (Mill Valley, CA: Nataraj Publishing, 1993), 77.

"USDA's Continuing Survey of Food Intakes by Individuals 1994–1996, 1999," from www.usda.gov

Chapter 2

A. Rosengren, K. Orth-Gomér, H. Wedel, and L. Wilhelmsen, "Stressful Life Events, Social Support, and Mortality in Men Born in 1933," British Medical Journal 307(6912) (1993): 1102–1105.

American Psychological Association Newsletter (January 26, 2012). The full report can be accessed at http://www.apa.org/news/press/releases/2012/01/chronic-disease.aspx

Avshalom Caspi, et al., "Influence of Life Stress on Depression: Moderation by a Polymorphism in the 5-HTT," Gene Science 301, no. 5631 (18 July 2003): 386–389.

B. S. McEwen, "Hormones and the Nervous System," Advances 7, no. 1 (1990): 50–54.

Bryan E. Robinson, "Are You a Work Addict?" East/West (August 1990): 50.

C. J. C. Hellman, et al., "A Study of the Effectiveness of Two Group Behavioral Medicine Interventions for Patients with Psychosomatic Complaints," Behavioral Medicine 16 (1990): 165–173.

Diane Fassel, "Work- and Rushaholics: Spotting a Lethal Disease," Longevity (September 1990): 78.

E. J. H. Mulder, et al, "Prenatal Maternal Stress: Effects on Pregnancy and the (Unborn) Child," Early Human Development (2002)70:3–14.

G. Holtmann, R. Kriebel, and M. V. Singer, "Mental Stress and Gastric Acid Secretion: Do Personality Traits Influence the Response?" Editor's Citation Abstract 35, no. 8 (1990): 998–1007.

Gailen D. Marshall and Sitesh R. Roy, "Stress and Allergic Diseases," pp. 799–818 in Robert Ader, ed., Psychoneuroimmunology, 4th ed., vol. 2 (New York: Elsevier, Inc., 2007), 815.

H. J. F. Baltrush, reported at the Third International Symposium on Detection and Prevention of Cancer, New York, April 16–May 1, 1976.

H. J. McQuay, et al., "Sytematic Review of Outpatient

Services for Chronic Pain Control," Health Technological Assessment 1 (1997): i–iv, 1–135; C. Redillas and S. Solomon, "Prophylactic Pharmacological Treatment of Chronic Daily Headache," Headache 40 (2000): 83–102; A. G. Lipman, "Analgesic for Neuropathic and Sympathetically Maintained Pain," Clinics in Geriatric Medicine 12 (1996): 501–515.

Hugo D. Critchley, et al., "Mental Stress and Sudden Cardiac Death: Asymmetric Midbrain Activity as a Linking Mechanism," Brain (2004) 128:75–85.

I. K. Crombie, M. B. Kenicer, W. C. S. Smith, and H. D. Tunstall-Pedoe, "Unemployment, Socioenvironmental Factors, and Coronary Heart Disease in Scotland," British Heart Journal (1989) 61:172–177.

L. M. Bellini and J. A. Shea Baime, "Variation of Mood and Empathy During Internship," Journal of the American Medical Association (2002) 287: 3143–3146.

Lynne C. Huffman and Rebecca del Carmen, "Prenatal Stress," in L. Eugene Arnold, ed., Childhood Stress (New York: John Wiley and Sons, Inc., 1990), 144–172.

M. Boles, B. Pelletier, and W. Lynch, "The Relationship Between Health Risks and Work Productivity," Journal of Occupational and Environmental Medicine 46, no. 7 (July 2004): 737–745. Also W. N. Burton, et al., "The Association of Medical Conditions and Presenteeism," Journal of Occupational and Environmental Medicine 46, no. 6 Suppl. (June 2004): S38–45.

M. Boles, B. Pelletier, and W. Lynch, "The Relationship between Health Risks and Work Productivity," Journal of Occupational and Environmental Medicine (2004): 46:737–745.

Marjory Roberts, "Stress and the Silent Heart Attack," Psychology Today (August 1987): 7.

Quoted in P. J. Rosch, "Stress and Cardiovascular Disease," Comprehensive Therapy (1983) 9(10): 6–13.

R. C. Chapman, R. P. Tuckett, and C. W. Song, "Pain and Stress in a Systems Perspective: Reciprocal Neural, Endocrine and Immune Interactions," Journal of Pain 9 (2008):122–145.

S. A. Washburn, Menopausal Medicine (1997) 5:5–8.

Sapolski is quoted in Jerry Lazar, "New Proof That Stress Ages the Brain," Longevity 2, no. 3 (1988): 25. Also see H. Fillit, "Stress, the Brain, Aging and Alzheimer's Disease: Long Term Effects of Stress on the Brain," Psychology Today, March 10, 2010.

Tori DeAngelis, "A Bright Future for PNI," Monitor on Psychology, 33:6 (June 2002). Accessed at http://www.apa.org/monitor/jun02/brightfuture.html

V. Maletic, et al. "Neurobiology of Depression: An Integrated View of New Findings," Clinical Practice 61, no. 12 (2007): 2030–2040. Also R. S. Duman, et al., Archives of General Psychiatry 54 (1997): 595–606; and P. S. Ericson, Acta Neurologica Scandinavia 110 (2004): 275–280

W. N. Burton, et al., "The Association of Medical Conditions and Presenteeism," Journal of Occupational and Environmental Medicine 46 (June, 2004): S38–45.

"Workplace Warning: Stress May Speed Brain Aging," New Sense Bulletin 16, no. 11 (1991): 1.

Chapter 3

Amy Mackey, "Power, Pessimism, and Prevention," http://www.units.muohio.edu/psybersite/control/health.shtml

Blair Justice, Who Gets Sick: Thinking and Health (Houston, TX: Peak Press, 1987), 61–62.

C. Conversano, A. Rotondo, E. Lensi, O. Della Vista, F. Arpone, and M. A. Reda, "Optimism and Its Impact on Mental and Physical Well-Being," Clinical Practice and Epidemiology in Mental Health, 6 (2010), 25–29.

C. S. Carver and M. F. Scheier, "Optimism," pp. 231–243 in C. R. Snyder and S. J. Lopez, eds., Handbook of Positive Psychology (London: Oxford University Press, 2002).

Caryle Hirshberg, "Spontaneous Remission: The Spectrum of Self-Repair," The Psychology of Health, Immunity, and Disease, vol. B, 186, in Proceedings of the Sixth International Conference of the National Institute for the Clinical Application of Behavioral Medicine (Mansfield Center, CT: NICABM).

Christopher Peterson and Mechele E. De Avila, "Optimistic Explanatory Style and the Perception of Health Problems," Journal of Clinical Psychology 51 (1):128–132, 2006.

Clive Wood, "Type-Casting: Is Disease Linked with Personality?" Nursing Times, 84, no. 48 (1988): 26.

Erika Waters, "Knowledge of Risk Perception and Behavior," State University at Buffalo, The State University of New York, December 2015.

Howard S. Friedman, The Self-Healing Personality (New York: Henry Holt and Company, 1991.
Jean M. Twenge, Liqing Zhang, and Charles Im, "It's Beyond My Control: A Cross-Temporal Meta-Analysis of Increasing Externality in Locus of Control, 1960–2002," Personality and Social Psychology Review 8, no. 3 (2004).

Judy Berlfein, "An Ill Nature," Psychology Today, n.d., 16.

Larry Dossey, Meaning and Medicine: A Doctor's Tales of Breakthrough and Healing (New York: Bantam Books, 1991), 16.

"Learned Helplessness," Emotional Competency, http://www.emotionalcompetency.com/helpless.htm

"Locus of Control and Cardiovascular Health," Job Stress Network, http://www.workhealth.org/risk/rfblocus.html

M. F. Scheier and C. S. Carver, "Optimism, Coping, and Health: Assessment and Implications of Generalized Outcome Expectancies," Health Psychology 4, no. 3 (1985): 219–247.

Martin E. P. Seligman, Learned Optimism (New York: Alfred A. Knopf, 1991).

"Mind over Cancer: An Exclusive Interview with Yale Surgeon Dr. Bernie Siegel," Prevention (March 1988): 59–64.

Nadine Smity, Anne Young, and Christina Lee, "Optimism, Health-Related Hardiness and Well-Being Among Older Australian Women," Journal of Health Psychology 9, no. 6 (2004): 741–752.

Pamela Williams-Piehota et al., "Matching Health Messages to Health Locus of Control Beliefs for Promoting Mammography Utilization," Psychology and Health 19, no. 4 (August 2004): 407–423.

Phillip L. Rice, Stress and Health: Principles and Practice for Coping and Wellness (Monterey, CA: Brooks/Cole Publishing Company, 1987), 109.

Phillip L. Rice, Stress and Health: Principles and Practice for Coping and Wellness (Monterey, CA: Brooks/Cole Publishing Company, 1987), 109.

S. C. Kobasa, S. R. Maddi, and S. Kahn, "Hardiness and Health: A Prospective Study," Journal of Personality and Social Psychology 42, no. 1 (1982):168–177.

Shimon Saphire-Bernstein, Baldwin M. Way, Heejung S. Kim, David K. Sherman, and Shelley E. Taylor, "Oxytocin Receptor Gene (OXTR) Is Related to Psychological Resources," Proceedings of the National Academy of Sciences, 108, no. 37 (September 13, 2011), 15118–15122.

W. Stelmach, K. Kaczmarczyk-Chalas, W. Bielecki, and W. Drygas, "The Association Between Income, Education, Control over Life and Health in a Large Urban Population of Poland," International Journal of Occupational Medicine & Environmental Health 17, no. 2 (2004): 299–310.

Chapter 4

A. Ohman, "Fear and Anxiety: Evolutionary, Cognitive, and Clinical Perspectives," pp. 573–593 in M. Lewis and J. M. Haviland-Jones, eds., Handbook of Emotions (New York: The Guilford Press, 2000).

A. Rozanski et al., "Mental Stress and the Induction of Silent Myocardial Ischemia in Patients with Coronary Artery Disease," New England Journal of Medicine 318 (1988): 1005–1012.

Anne H. Rosenfeld, "Depression: Dispelling Despair," Psychology Today 13, no. 3 (June 1985): 28.

Bert N. Uchino, "Social Support and Health: A Review of Physiological Processes Potentially Underlying Links to Disease Outcomes," Journal of Behavioral Medicine, 29, no. 4 (August 2006). See also Sheldon Cohen and S. Leonard Syme, eds., Social Support and Health (London: Academic Press, 1985).

Biing-Jiun Shen, et al., "Anxiety Characteristics Independently and Prospectively Predict Myocardial Infarction in Men: The Unique Contribution of Anxiety Among Psychologic Factors," Journal of the American College of Cardiology 51(2008): 113–119.

Blair Justice, Who Gets Sick: Thinking and Health (Houston, TX: Peak Press, 1987.

Cathy Perlmutter, "Conquer Chronic Worry," Prevention (November 1993): 76–80.

Christine Heim, et al., "Effect of Childhood Trauma on Adult Depression and Neuroendocrine Function: Sex-Specific Moderation by CRH Receptor 1 Gene," Frontiers in Behavioral Neuroscience 3, no. 41 (2009): 41. (Pre-published online 2009 August 16. doi: 10.3389/neuro.08.041.2009)

D. B. Larson, J. P. Swyers, and M. E. McCullough, eds., Scientific Research on Spirituality and Health: A Consensus Report (Rockville, MD: National Institute for Healthcare Research, 1998).

Depression Guideline Panel, Depression in Primary Care: Volume 2, Treatment of Major Depression, Clinical Practice Guideline Number 5 (Rockville, MD: U. S. Department of Health and Human Services, Agency for Healthcare Policy and Research (AHCPR), Publication no. 93–0551, 1993).

E. Harburg, M. Julius, N. Kaciroti, L. Gleiberman, and M. A. Schork, "Expressive/suppressive Anger-coping Responses, Gender, and Types of Mortality: A 17-year Follow-up (Tecumseh, Michigan, 1971–1988)," Psychosomatic Medicine 65, no. 4 (2003): 588–597.

E. L. Garland, B. Fredrickson, A. M. Kring, D. P. Johnson, P. S. Meyer, and D. L. Penn, "Upward Spirals of Positive Emotions Counter Downward Spirals of Negativity: Insights from the Broaden-and-Build Theory and Affective Neuroscience on the Treatment of Emotion Dysfunctions and Deficits in Psychopathology, Clinical Psychology Review 30, no. 7 (2010):849–864.

Emrika Padus, Positive Living and Health: The Complete Guide to Brain/Body Healing and Mental Empowerment

(Emmaus, PA: Rodale Press, 1990).

Examples are from Edward Dolnick, "Scared to Death," Hippocrates (March–April 1989): 106–108.

G. I. Keitner, et al., "12-Month Outcome of Patients with Major Depression and Comorbid Psychiatric or Mental Illness," American Journal of Psychiatry 148 (1991): 345–350; P. J. Lustman, L. S. Griffith, and R. E. Clouse, "Depression in Adults with Diabetes: Results of a Five-Year Follow-Up Study," Diabetes Care 11 (1988): 605–612; and R. M. Carney, et al., "Depression as a Risk Factor for Mortality after Acute Myocardial Infarction," American Journal of Cardiolology 92, no. 11 (2003): 1277–1281.

G. Ironson et al., "Effects of Anger on Left Ventricular Ejection Fraction in Coronary Artery Disease," American Journal of Cardiology 70 (1992): 281–285.

H. K. Manji, et al., "Enhancing Neuronal Plasticity and Cellular Resilience to Develop Novel, Improved Therapeutics for Difficult-to-Treat Depression," Biological Psychiatry 53 (2003): 707–742.

J. D. Bremer, et al., "Hippocampal Volume Reduction in Major Depression," American Journal of Psychiatry 157 (2000): 115–118.

J. P. Henry, J. P. Meehan, and P. M. Stephens, "The Use of Psychosocial Stimuli to Induce Prolonged Systolic Hypertension in Mice," Psychosomatic Medicine 29 (1967): 408–432; R. P. Forsyth, "Blood Pressure Responses to Long-Term Avoidance Schedules in the Restrained Rhesus Monkey," Psychosomatic Medicine 31 (1969): 300; and R. P. Forsyth, "Regional Blood Flow Changes During 72-Hour Avoidance Schedules in the Monkey," Science 173 (1971): 546.

J. R. Peteet and H. G. Prigerson, "Religiousness and Spiritual Support among Advanced Cancer Patients and Associations with End-of- life Treatment Preferences and Quality of Life," Journal of Clinical Oncology 25 (2007), 555-560.

James W. Pennebaker and Harald C. Traue, "Inhibition and Psychosomatic Processes," in Harald C. Traue and James W. Pennebaker, eds., Emotion Inhibition and Health (Seattle, WA: Hogrefe & Huber Publishers, 1993), 152–153.

Jennifer E. Graham, Lisa M. Christian, and Janice K. Kiecolt-Glaser, "Close Relationships and Immunity," p. 781 in Robert Ader, ed., Psychoneuroimmunology, 4th ed., vol. 2 (New York: Elsevier, Inc., 2007).

John Shavers, The Identification of Depression and Anxiety in a Medical Outpatient Setting and Their Correlation to Presenting Physical Complaints (PhD dissertation, University of Utah, 1996).

Ken Wilber, A Brief History of Everything (Shambhala: 2nd edition 2001); Eckhart Tolle: The New Earth: Awakening

to Your Life's Purpose (New York: Plume: 2006).

L. D. Kubzansky et al., "Angry Breathing: A Prospective Study of Hostility and Lung Function in the Normative Aging Study," Thorax, October 2006. See also S. Cohen, D. A. Tyrell, and A. P. Smith, "Psychological Stress and Susceptibility to the Common Cold," New England Journal of Medicine 325 (1991): 606–612.

L.S. Linn and J. Yager, "Recognition of Depression and Anxiety by Primary Care Physicians," Psychosomatics 25 (1984): 593–595, 599–600.

Larry Dossey, Meaning and Medicine: A Doctor's Tales of Breakthrough and Healing (New York: Bantam Books, 1991), 158–159.

M. A. Jansen and L. R. Muenz, "A Retrospective Study of Personality Variables Associated with Fibrocystic Disease and Breast Cancer," Journal of Psychosomatic Research 28 (1984): 35–42.

M. A. Mittleman et al., "Educational Attainment, Anger, and the Risk of Triggering Myocardial Infarction Onset," Archives of Internal Medicine 157 (1997): 769–775.

M. Friedman and D. Ulmer, Treating Type A Behavior and Your Heart (New York: Fawcett, 1984). See also the summary of these practices in Diane K. Ulmer, "Helping the Coronary Patient Reduce Hostility and Hurry Sickness: A Structured Behavioral Group Approach," The Psychology of Health, Immunity, and Disease, vol. A, in Proceedings of the Sixth International Conference of the National Institute for the Clinical Application of Behavioral Medicine, Hilton Head Island, South Carolina, December, 1994, 592.

M. Kumar et al., "Homocysteine Decreases Blood Flow to the Brain due to Vascular Resistance in Carotid Artery," Neurochemistry International 2008 [E-publication ahead of print].

M. W. Ketterer, G. Mahr, and A. D. Goldberg, "Psychological Factors Affecting a Medical Condition: Ischemic Coronary Heart Disease," Journal of Psychosomatic Research 48, nos. 4–5 (2000): 357–367.

Martin Rossman, quoted in Will Stapp, "Imagine Yourself Well," Medical Self-Care (January–February 1988): 27–30.

"Mind over Cancer: An Exclusive Interview with Yale Surgeon Dr. Bernie Siegel," Prevention (March 1988): 59–64.

N. Lee Smith and John Shavers, "Physical Symptoms Highly Predictive of Depression and Anxiety," presented at the American Psychosomatic Society annual meeting; Psychosomatic Medicine APS abstracts 1996.

Nadine Smith, Anne Young, and Christina Lee, "Optimism, Health-Related Hardiness and Well-Being Among Older Australian Women," Journal of Health Psychology 9, no. 6 (2004): 741–752.

Redford B. Williams, "Conferences with Patients and Doctors: A 69-Year-Old Man with Anger and Angina," Journal of the American Medical Association 282 (August 25, 1999): 8.

Redford Williams and Virginia Williams, Anger Kills (New York: Random House/Times Books, 1993).

Robert Ornstein and David Sobel, "The Healing Brain," Psychology Today, March 1987, 48–52.

Robert S. Eliot, Is It Worth Dying For? How to Make Stress Work For You—Not Against You (Bantam, 1989).

Robert Spitzer et al., Diagnostic and Statistical Manual IV (Washington, DC: American Psychiatric Association, 1998).

S. Cohen, B. H. Gottlieb, and L. G. Underwood, "Social Relationships and Health," pp. 3–25 in S. Cohen, L. G. Underwood, and B. H. Gottlieb, eds., Measuring and Intervening in Social Support (New York: Oxford University Press, 2000).

S. Kennedy, J. Kiecolt-Glaser, and R. Glaser, "Immunological Consequences of Acute and Chronic Stressors: Mediating Role of Interpersonal Relationships," British Journal of Medical Psychology 61 (1988): 77–85.

See the discussion of anxiety disorders at the National institutes of Health website, accessed at http://www.nimh.nih.gov/health/topics/anxiety-disorders/index.shtml

Steven Locke and Douglas Colligan, The Healer Within: The New Medicine of Mind and Body (New York: E. P. Dutton, 1986), 183.

T. D. Borkovec, E. Robinson, T. Pruzinsky, and J. A. DePree, "Preliminary Exploration of Worry: Some Characteristics and Processes, Behaviour Research and Therapy 21(1983): 9–16.

T. Koike et al., "Raised Homocysteine and Low Folate and Vitamin B-12 Concentrations Predict Cognitive Decline in Community-Dwelling Older Japanese Adults," Clinical Nutrition 2008 [E-publication ahead of print].
T. W. Smith, "Hostility and Health: Current Status of a Psychometric Hypothesis," Health Psychology 11 (1992): 139–150.

"Toxic Marriage May (Literally) Hurt Your Heart," Associated Press, reporting on studies cited in Archives of Internal Medicine, October 8, 2007.

Chapter 5

Alix Kerr, "Hearts Need Friends," Physician's Weekly, (n.d.).

"Americans Marrying Older, Living Alone More, See Households Shrinking, Census Bureau Reports," U.S. Census Bureau News, May 25, 2006.

Anne F. Young, Anne Russell, and Jennifer R. Powers, "The Sense of Belonging to a Neighbourhood: Can It Be Measured and Is It Related to Health and Well Being in Older Women?" Social Sciences and Medicine 59, no. 12 (December 2004): 2627–2637.

Brent Q. Hafen and Kathryn J. Frandsen, People Who Need People (Natick, MA: Cordillera Press, 1987).

C. E. Depner and B. Ingersoll-Dayton, "Supportive Relationships in Later Life," Psychology and Aging 3, no. 4 (December 1988): 348–357.

Carin Rubenstein and Phillip Shaver, "Are You Lonely? How to Find Intimacy, Love, and Happiness," Shape (August 1987), 72.

Carol D. Ryff and Burton H. Singer, "Introduction: Integrating Emotion into the Study of Social Relationships and Health," in Ryff and Singer, Emotion, Social Relationships, and Health (New York: Oxford University Press, 2001).

"Census: More Americans Living Alone," USA Today, September 2, 2005.

Charlotte A. Schoenborn, "Marital Status and Health: United States 1999–2002," Centers for Disease Control, Advance Data from Vital and Health Statistics 351 (Dec. 15, 2004).

Chris Segrin and Stacey Passalacqua, "Functions of Loneliness, Social Support, Health Behaviors, and Stress in Assocation with Poor Health," Health Communication, 25 (4), 2010, 312.

D. Askt, "A Talk with John Cacciopo: A Chicago Scientist Suggests that Loneliness Is a Threat to Your Health," The Boston Globe, accessed at http://www.boston.com/bostonglobe/ideas/articles/2008/09/21/a-_talk_with_john_cacioppo/

D. B. Hudson, S. M. Elek, and C. Campbell-Gorssman, "Depression, Self-Esteem, Loneliness, and Social Support Among Adolescent Mothers Participating in the New Parents Project," Adolescence 35, no. 139 (Autumn 2000), 445–453.

David Spiegel and Rachel Kimerling, "Group Psychotherapy for Women with Breast Cancer: Relationships Among Social Support, Emotional Expression, and Survival," pp. 196–197 in Carol D. Ryff and Burton H. Singer, eds., Emotion, Social Relationships, and Health (New York: Oxford University Press, 2001).

Deborah Preston and Jorge Grimes, "A Study of Differences in Social Support," Journal of Gerontological Nursing 13, no. 2 (2003): 36–40.

"Domestic Migration Across Regions, Divisions, and States: 1995 to 2000," Census 2000 Special Reports (August 2003), 1.

Frances Sheridan Goulart, "How to Live a Longer, Healthier Life," (n.p., n.d.).

Glenn T. Stanton, "Only a Piece of Paper? How Marriage Improves Adult Health," Divorce Statistics Collection—Smart Marriages Archive, http://www.palmettofamily.org/viewarticle.asp?ID=10

H. Morowitz, "Hiding in the Hammond Report," Hospital Practice (August 1975), 35–39.

Harry T. Reis, "Relationship Experiences and Emotional Well-Being," in Carol D. Ryff and Burton H. Singer, eds., Emotion, Social Relationships, and Health (New York: Oxford University Press, 2001).

J. F. Helliwell and R. D. Putnam, "The Social Context of Well-Being," Philosophical Transactions of the Royal Society of London. Series B: Biological Sciences 359, no. 1149 (September 2004): 1435–1436.

J. R. Vicary and D. A. Corneal, "A Comparison of Young Women's Psychosocial Status Based on Age of Their First Childbirth," Family Community Health 24, no. 2 (July 2001), 73–84.

J. S. House, Work Stress and Social Support (Reading, MA: Addison-Wesley, 1981).

J. T. Cacioppo, J. H. Fowler, and N. A. Christakis, "Alone in the Crowd: The Structure and Spread of Loneliness in a Large Social Network," Journal of Personality and Social Psychology, 97 (December 2009).

James Pennebaker, Opening Up: The Healing Power of Confiding in Others (New York: William Morrow and Company, 1990), 71.

Jennifer E. Graham, Lisa M. Christian, and Janice K. Kiecolt-Glaser, "Close Relationships and Immunity," p. 781 in Robert Ader, ed., Psychoneuroimmunology, 4th ed., vol. 2 (New York: Elsevier, Inc., 2007).

John Cacioppo, "Biological Costs of Social Stress in the Elderly," paper delivered at a meeting of the American Psychological Association, Washington, DC, August 6, 2000.

Julianne Holt-Lunstad, Timothy B. Smith, and J. Bradley Layton, "Social Relationships and Mortality Risk: A Meta-analytic Review," PLoS Medicine 7, no. 7 (2010).

Kenneth Pelletier, Sound Mind, Sound Body: A New Model for Lifelong Health (New York: Simon & Schuster, 1994), 137–138.

L. Hawkley, Current Directions in Psychological Science, vol. 16, August 2007, 187–191.

L.C. Gallo et al., "Socioeconomic Status, Resources, Psychological Experiences, and Emotional Responses: A Test of the Reserve Capacity Model," Journal of Personality and Social Psychology 88 (2005): 386–399.

Lori J. Curtis, Martin D. Dooley, and Shelley A. Phipps, "Child Well-Being and Neighbourhood Quality: Evidence from the Canadian National Longitudinal Survey of Children and Youth," Social Sciences and Medicine 58, no. 10 (May 2004): 1917–1927.

Louise Bernikow, Alone in America (New York: Harper & Row, 1986), 18.

Louise Hawkley and John Cacioppo, "Loneliness and Its Effects on Health," Current Directions in Psychological Science (August 2007).

M. E. Lachman and S. Agrigoroaei, "Promoting Functional Health in Midlife and Old Age: Long-Term Protective Effects of Control Beliefs, Social Support, and Physical Exercise," PLoS ONE, 5, no 10 (2010).

M. W. Verheijden, J. C. Bakx, C. van Weel, M. A. Koelen, and W. A. van Staveren, "Role of Social Support in Lifestyle-Focused Weight Management Interventions," European Journal of Clinical Nutrition, 59, supplement 1 (2005).

Marc Pilisuk and Susan Hillier Parks, The Healing Web (Hanover, NH: University Press of New England, 1986).

MayoClinic.com, "Developing Social Support: How to Cultivate a Network of Friends to Help You Through Rough Times," http://www.cnn.com/HEALTH/library/MH/00041.html

Meredith Minkler, "The Social Component of Health," American Journal of Health Promotion (Fall 1986): 33–38.

Miranda Hitti, "The Health Perks of Marriage," WebMD Medical News, http://www.webmd.com/balance/news/20041215/health-perks-of-marriage

"Most Senior Citizens Experience Loneliness, Say Researchers," SeniorJournal.com, from www.rotaryclubofsantamonica.org/In%20The%20News/2002-2003/seniorjournaldotcom.htm, posted November 21, 2005.

Nancy Shute, "Why Loneliness Is Bad for Your Health: A Conversation with John Cacioppo," U. S. News and World Report, November 12, 2008; see also A. Steptoe, N. Owen, S. R. Kunz-Ebrecht, and L. Brydon, "Loneliness and Neuroendocrine, Cardiovascular, and Inflammatory Stress Responses in Middle-Aged Men and Women," Psychoneuroendocrinology 29, no. 5 (June 2004), 593–611.

Pirkko E. Routasalo et al., "Social Contacts and Their Relationship to Loneliness Among Aged People—A Population-Based Study," Gerontology 52 (2006), 181–187.

"Psychologist John Cacioppo Explains Why Loneliness Is Bad for Your Health," Institute for Genomics and Systems Biology, January 25, 2011, accessed from http://www.igsb.org/news/psychologist-john-cacioppo-explains-why-loneliness-is-bad-for-health.htm

Robin Tricoles, "Making the Connections between Loneliness and Health," FABBS Foundation, March 7, 2012, accessed from http://www.fabbs.org/fabbs-foundation/science-communications/making-the-connections-between-loneliness-and-health/

S. Kennedy, J. Kiecolt-Glaser, and R. Glaser, "Immunological Consequences of Acute and Chronic Stressors: Mediating Role of Interpersonal Relationships," British Journal of Medical Psychology 61 (1988): 77–85.

Sharon Faelten, David Diamond, and the editors of Prevention magazine, Take Control of Your Life: A Complete Guide to Stress Relief (Emmaus, PA: Rodale Press, 1988), 58.

Sheldon Cohen, "Social Relationships and Susceptibility to the Common Cold," in Carol D. Ryff and Burton H. Singer, eds., Emotion, Social Relationships, and Health (New York: Oxford University Press, 2001).

"Surviving a Heart Attack: Emotional Support Is Key," Mental Medicine Update (Spring 1993): 2.

Susan L. Duncan, "Loneliness: A Health Hazard of Modern Times," Interactions, 13 (1), 1995, 5–9.

T. Koropeckyj-Cox, "Loneliness and Depression in Middle and Old Age: Are the Childless More Vulnerable?" Journals of Gerontology Series B Psychological Sciences and Social Sciences 53, no. 6 (November 1998), S303–312.

Terrence L. Amick and Judith K. Ockene, "The Role of Social Support in the Modification of Risk Factors for Cardiovascular Disease," pp. 260–261 in Sally A. Shumaker and Susan M. Czajkowski, eds., Social Support and Cardiovascular Disease (New York: Plenum Press, 1994).

The editors of Prevention magazine, Positive Living and Health: The Complete Guide to Brain/Body Healing and Mental Empowerment (Emmaus, PA: Rodale Press, 1990), 154.

Todd Jackson, "Relationships Between Perceived Close Social Support and Health Practices within Community Samples of American Women and Men," Journal of Psychology, 140, no. 3 (2006), 229–246.

Tom Ferguson, "The Invisible Health Care System," from http://www.healthy.net/scr/Article.asp?Id=1016, January–February 1988.

W. M. Troxel, K. A. Matthews, L. C. Gallo, and L. H. Kuller,

"Marital Quality and Occurrence of the Metabolic Syndrome in Women," Archives of Internal Medicine, 165 (2005), 1022–1027.

"You're Not Alone When It Comes to Loneliness," Harvard Health Letter 24, no. 7 (1999), 4.

Chapter 6

"Activation of Brain Region Predicts Altruism," Health News Today (St. Paul, MN, January 21, 2007).

Albert Schweitzer, quoted by F. Charatan, "The Doctor Within," British Medical Journal 328 (2004), 1426.

Allan Luks, "Helper's High," Psychology Today (October 1988), 39–42.

Allan Luks, The Healing Power of Doing Good (New York: Fawcett, 1992), 80–81.

Allan Luks and Peggy Payne, The Healing Power of Doing Good (New York: Fawcett Columbine, 1992).

American Psychological Association, "Stress Affects Immunity in Ways Related to Stress Type and Duration, As Shown by Nearly 300 Studies," http://www.apa.org/releases/stress_immune. html, July 4, 2004 (revised 2007).

Bernie Siegel, Love, Medicine and Miracles, (New York: Harper and Row, 1986), 41.

Bernie Siegel, Peace, Love, and Healing (New York: Harper & Row, 1989).

Bruno Cortis, "Spirituality and Medicine," in Proceedings of the Fourth National Conference on the Psychology of Health, Immunity, and Disease, held at Hilton Head Island, SC, December 1992 (Mansfield Center, CT: The National Institute for the Clinical Application of Behavioral Medicine: 1992).

C. Schwartz, J. B. Meisenhelder, Y. Ma, and G. Reed, Psychosomatic Medicine 65 (2003), 778–785.

Carolyn Schwartz, Janice Bell Meisenhelder, Yunsheng Ma, and George Reed, "Altruistic Social Interest Behaviors Are Associated With Better Mental Health," Psychosomatic Medicine, 65 (2003): 778–85.

"Compassion RX: The Many Health Benefits of Altruism," Earthpages.org, http://epages.wordpress.com/2007/10/26/compassion-rx-the-many-health-benefits-of-altruism

D. A. Matthews and D. B. Larson, The Faith Factor, Volume III: Enhancing Life Satisfaction (Rockville, MD: National Institute for Healthcare Research, 1995).

D. B. Larson, J. P. Swyers, and M. E. McCullough, eds.,

Scientific Research on Spirituality and Health: A Consensus Report (Rockville, MD: National Institute for Healthcare Research, 1998).

D. Jost, et al., American Heritage Dictionary of the English Language, 4th edition (Boston: Houghton Mifflin, 2006).

David Sloan Wilson and Mihaly Czikszentmihalyi, "Health and the Ecology of Altruism," in Stephen G. Post, ed., The Science of Altruism and Health (Oxford, UK: Oxford University Press, 2007).

Deepak Chopra: The Seven Spiritual Laws of Success: A Practical Guide to the Fulfillment of Your Dreams (New World Library / Amber-Allen Publishing: 1994), 13.

Diane Swanbrow, "People Who Give Live Longer, IRS Study Shows," The University Record Online, http://www.umich.edu/~urecord/0102/Nov18_02/15.shtml

E. G. Diamond, C. F. Kittle, and J. E. Crockett, "Evaluation of Internal Mammary Artery Ligation and Sham Procedure in Angina Pectoris," Circulation 18 (1958), 712–713.

Eileen Rockefeller Growald and Allan Luks, "Beyond Self," American Health (March 1988), 51–3.

Esther M. Sternberg, "Approaches to Defining Mechanisms by Which Altruistic Love Affects Health," The Institute for Research on Unlimited Love, http://www.unlimitedloveinstitute.org/ publications/pdf/whitepapers/Mechanisms_Altruistic.pdf

G. Ironson, et al., Annals of Behavioral Medicine 24 (2002), 34¬–48.

Glenn E. Richardson and Melody Powers Noland, "Treating the Spiritual Dimension Through Educational Imagery," Health Values 8, no. 6 (1984), 28.

Gregg D. Jacobs, "Clinical Applications of the Relaxation Response and Mind-Body Interventions," Journal of Alternative and Complementary Medicine, 7, no. 1 (December 2001): 93–101.

Harvard Mind/Body Institute Symposium: "Spirituality and Healing in Medicine," Salt Lake City, May 2002.

Herbert Benson and D. P. McCallie, "Angina Pectoris and the Placebo Effect," New England Journal of Medicine 300, no. 25 (1979), 1424–1429.

J. A. Blumenthal, et al., "Stress Management and Exercise Training in Cardiac Patients with Myocardial Ischemia: Effects on prognosis and evaluation of mechanisms." Archives of Internal Medicine 157 (1997), 2213–2223.

J. Kong, et al., "Placebo Analgesia: Findings from Brain Imaging Studies and Emerging Hypotheses," Reviews in Neuroscience 18, no. 3/4 (2007), 173–190. Also, K. Wiech, M. Ploner, and I. Tracey, "Neurocognitive Aspects of Pain Perception," Trends in Cognitive Science 12, no. 8 (August 2008), 306–313.

J. Primavera, "The Unintended Consequences of Volunteerism: Positive Outcomes for Those Who Serve," Journal of Prevention and Intervention in the Community 18 (1999): 1–2.

J. R. Peteet and H. G. Prigerson, "Religiousness and Spiritual Support among Advanced Cancer Patients and Associations with End-of- life Treatment Preferences and Quality of Life," Journal of Clinical Oncology 25 (2007), 555-560.

Jerome D. Frank, "Emotional Reactions of American Soldiers to an Unfamiliar Disease," American Journal of Psychiatry 102 (1946), 631–640.

Joan Borysenko, Minding the Body, Mending the Mind (Reading, MA: Addison-Wesley Publishing Company, 1987), 10.

K. Pelletier, "The Spirit of Health," Advances: Journal of the Institute for the Advancement of Health 5, no. 4 (1988), 4.

Kathleen Hall, "Stress Reducing Tips," The Stress Institute, 2005.

Kirsti A. Dyer, "The Health Benefits of Altruism—How Giving Back Is Good for You" (2012), retrieved from http://www.squidoo.com/altruism

Larry S. Chapman, "Developing a Useful Perspective on Spiritual Health: Love, Joy, Peace, and Fulfillment," American Journal of Health Promotion (Fall 1987), 12.

Michele Dillon, "Is It Good to Do Good? Altruism and Health," A University Dialogue on Health 2009–2010.

P. Dulin and R. Hill, Aging and Mental Health 7 (2003), 294–299.

Pamela G. Reed, "Spirituality and Well-Being in Terminally Ill Hospitalized Adults," Research in Nursing and Health 10 (1987), 335–344.

Paul Pearsall, Super Joy (New York: Doubleday, 1988).

Phillip J. Waite, Steven R. Hawks, and Julie A. Gast, "The Correlation Between Spiritual Well-Being and Health Behaviors," American Journal of Health Promotion 13, no. 3 (January/February 1999), 159–162.

Samuel Oliner and Piotr Olaf Zylicz, Altruism, Intergroup Apology, Forgiveness, and Reconciliation (St. Paul, MN: Paragon House, 2008).

Sarah Lang, "Extend Your Hand, Extend Your Life," Longevity (March 1989), 18.

Shu Pang, "Is Altruism Good for the Altruistic Giver?" The Dartmouth Undergraduate Journal of Science online, Spring 2009, accessed at http://dujs.dartmouth.edu/spring-2009/is-altruism-good-for-the-altruistic-giver

Stanley H. Block: Come to Your Senses: Demystifying the Mind-Body Connection (Hillsboro, OR: Beyond Words Publishing: 2005).

Stephen G. Post, "Altruism, Happiness, and Health: It's Good to Be Good," International Journal of Behavioral Medicine, 12, no. 2 (2005), 66–77.

Stephen G. Post, "It's Good to Be Good: 2011 Fifth Annual Scientific Report on Health, Happiness and Helping Others," The International Journal of Person Centered Medicine, 1, no. 4 (2011).

Stewart Wolf, "The Pharmacology of Placebos," Pharmacological Reviews II (1959), 689–704.

Tamar Nordenberg, "The Healing Power of Placebos," FDA Consumer (January/February 2000), 14–17.

Viktor E. Frankl, Man's Search for Meaning (New York: Pocket Books, 1997) (first published, 1946).

Chapter 7

A. A. Shaheen, et al., "Effect of Pretreatment with Vitamin E or Diazepam on Brain Metabolism of Stressed Rats," Journal of Biochemistry Pharmacology 46 (1993), 194.

A. Baumgartner , et al., "Neuroendocrinological Evaluations During Sleep Deprivation in Depression. I. Early Morning Levels of Thyrotropin, TH, Cortisol, Prolactin, LH, FSH, Estradiol, and Testosterone," Biological Psychiatry 28 (1990), 556–568; A. Baumgartner, D. Riemann, and M. Berger, "Neuroendocrinological Evaluations During Sleep Deprivation in Depression. II. Longitudinal Measurement of Thyrotropin, TH, Cortisol, Prolactin, GH and LH During Sleep and Sleep Deprivation," Biological Psychiatry 28 (1990), 569–587; and M. H. Bonnet, "Acute Sleep Deprivation," pp. 56–57 M. H. Kryger, T. Roth, and W. C. Dement, eds., Principles and Practice of Sleep Medicine (Philadelphia, PA: Elsevier Saunders, 2005).

A. H. Calhoun, et al., "The Prevalence and Spectrum of Sleep Problems in Women with Transformed Migraine," Headache 46, no. 4 (April 2006), 604–610.

B. M. Cohen and A. L. Miller, "Lecithin in Mania," American Journal of Psychiatry 137 (1980), 242; and S. Delion, S. Chalon, and D. Guilloteau, "Age-Related Changes in Phospholipid Fatty Acid Composition and Monoaminergic Neurotransmission in the Hippocampus of Rats Fed a Balanced or an N-3 Polyunsaturated Fatty Acid-deficient Diet," Journal of Lipid Research 38 (1997), 680.

C. A. Everson, "Sustained Sleep Deprivation Impairs Host Defense," American Journal of Physiology 265, 5, pt. 2 (1993), R1148–54.

C. A. Everson and T. A. Wehr, "Nutritional and Metabolic Adaptations in Prolonged Sleep Deprivation in the Rat," American Journal of Physiology 264, 2, pt. 2 (1993), R376–87.

C. L. Whelton, I. Salit, and H. Moldofsky, "Sleep, Epstein-Barr Virus Infection, Musculoskeletal Pain and Depressive Symptoms in Chronic Fatigue Syndrome," Journal of Rheumatology 19 (1992), 939–943.

D. F. Dinges, N. L. Rogers, and M. D. Baynard, "Chronic Sleep Deprivation," pp. 67–76 in M. H. Kryger, T. Roth, and W. C. Dement, eds., Principles and Practice of Sleep Medicine (Philadelphia, PA: Elsevier Saunders, 2005).

D. Kritchevsky, "Diet and Cancer: What Is Next?" Journal of Nutrition 133 (2003), 386s.

D. Leger, "The Cost of Sleep-Related Accidents: A Report for the National Commission on Sleep Disorders Research," Sleep 17 (1994), 84–93; and A. I. Pack, "The Prevalence of Work-Related Sleep Problems," Journal of General Internal Medicine 10 (1995), 57.

E. M. Taveras, et al., "Short Sleep Duration in Infancy and Risk of Childhood Overweight, Archives of Pediatrics and Adolescent Medicine 162 (2008), 305–311.

F. Hohagen, et al., "Prevalence and Treatment of Insomnia in General Practice: A Longitudinal Study," European Archives of Psychiatry and Clinical Neuroscience 242 (1993), 329–336.

H. Moldofsky, "Sleep and Fibrositis Syndrome," Rheumatic Disease Clinics of North America 15 (1989), 91–103. Also H. Moldofsky, "Fibromyalgia, Sleep Disorder and Chronic Fatigue Syndrome," CIBA Foundation Symposium 173 (1993), 262–279; and H. Moldofsky, P. Scarsbrick, R. England, and H. Smythe, "Musculoskeletal Symptoms and Non-REM Sleep Disturbance in Patients with 'Fibrositis Syndrome' and Healthy Subjects," Psychosomatic Medicine 37(1975), 341–351.

H. Moldofsky, et al., "Induction of Neurasthenic Musculoskeletal Pain Syndrome by Selective Deep Sleep Stage Deprivation," Psychosomatic Medicine 38 (1976), 35–44.

J. M. Starr, J. Wardlaw, and K. Ferguson, "Increased Blood Brain Barrier Permeability in Type II Diabetes Demonstrated by Gadolinium Magnetic Resonance Imaging," Journal of Neurology, Neurosurgery & Psychiatry 74 (2003), 70.

J. R. Davidson, K. Abraham and K. M. Connor, "Effectiveness of Chromium in Atypical Depression, a Placebo-Controlled Trial," Biological Psychiatry 53 (2003), 261.

M. H. Bonnet, "Acute Sleep Deprivation," pp. 56–68 in

M. H. Kryger, T. Roth, and W. C. Dement, eds. Principles and Practice of Sleep Medicine. (Philadelphia, PA: Elsevier Saunders, 2005).

M. Kuppermann, et al., "Sleep Problems and Their Correlates in a Working Population," Journal of General Internal Medicine 10 (1995), 25–32.
Marvin R. Brown and Laurel A. Fisher, "Brain Peptides and Intercellular Messengers," Journal of the American Medical Association 251 (10): 1310–14.

"Micronutrients for Older Adults," Linus Pauling Institute, Oregon State University, http://lpi.oregonstate.edu/infocenter/olderadultnut.html

N. Breslau, R. B. Lipton, and W. F. Stewart, "Comorbidity of Migraine and Depression: Investigating Potential Etiology and Therapy," Journal of Neurology 60 (2003), 1308.

N. L. Smith, "Physical Symptoms Highly Predictive of Depression and Anxiety," American Psychosomatic Society annual meeting, Williamsburg, Virginia, May 8–10, 1996, Psychosomatic Medicine abstracts 1996, and J. Shavers, The Identification of Depression and Anxiety in a Medical Outpatient Setting and Their Correlation to Presenting Physical Complaints (PhD dissertation, University of Utah, 1996).

National Sleep Foundation, 2005 Sleep in America Poll (Washington, DC: National Sleep Foundation; 2005); http://www.sleepfoundation.org/_content/hottopics/2005_summary_of_findings.pdf A. I. Pack, "The Prevalence of Work-Related Sleep Problems," Journal of General Internal Medicine 10 (1995), 57. Also see Gallup Organization, Sleep in America: A National Survey of U. S. Adults (Washington, DC: National Sleep Foundation, 1991).; M. B. Balter and E. H. Uhlenhuth, "New Epidemiological Findings About Insomnia and Its Treatment," Journal of Clinical Psychiatry 53, suppl. (1992), 34–43; P. K. Schweitzer, et al., "Consequences of Reported Poor Sleep," Sleep Research 21 (1992), abstract, 2; and M. S. Aldrich, "Automobile Accidents in Patients with Sleep Disorders," Sleep 12 (1989), 487–494.

P. D'Eufemia, M. Cell, and R. Finocchiaro, "Abnormal Intestinal Permeability in Children with Autism," Acta Pædiatrica 85 (1996), 1076.

P. Lavie, "Sleep Habits and Sleep Disturbances in Industrial Workers in Israel: Main Findings and Some Characteristics of Workers Complaining of Excessive Daytime Sleepiness," Sleep 4 (1981), 147–158.

R. C. Hall and J. R. Joffe, "Hypomagnesemia. Physical and Psychiatric Symptoms," Journal of the American Medical Association 224 (1973), 1749.

R. J. Wurtman and J. J. Wurtman, "Carbohydrates and Depression," Scientific American 260 (1989), 68.

Shaheen E. Lakhan and Karen F. Vieira, "Nutritional Therapies for Mental Disorders," Nutrition Journal 7, no. 2 (2008).

Shirley Vanderbilt, "Food: Your Body's Natural Healer," Body Sense (Spring/Summer 2007), 37.

Stoller, "Economic Effects of Insomnia," and S. Weyerer and H. Dilling, "Prevalence and Treatment of Insomnia in the Community: Results From the Upper Bavarian Field Study," Sleep 14 (1991), 392–8; J. D. Kales , et al., "Biopsychobehavioral Correlates of Insomnia. V. Clinical Characteristics and Behavioral Correlates," American Journal of Psychiatry 141 (1984), 1371–6. Similar results were found in L. C. Johnson and C. L. Spinweber, "Quality of Sleep and Performance in the Navy: A Longitudinal Study of Poor Sleepers," pp. 13–28 in C. Guilleminault and E. Lugaresi, eds., Sleep/Wake Disorders: Natural History, Epidemiology and Long Term Evolution (New York: Raven Press, 1983).

"The Relationship between Nutrition and Mental Disorders," Science Magazine 2008, doi.876302637749706209

"USDA's Continuing Survey of Food Intakes by Individuals 1994–1996, 1999," from www.usda.gov.

Chapter 8

Abraham Maslow, Personality and Motivation (HarperCollins Publishers; 3 Sub. edition 1987), Chapter 11.

Charles Garfield, Peak Performers (New York: Harper Paperbacks, 1987).

D. C. McClelland, G. Ross, and V. Patel, "The Effects of an Academic Examination on Salivary Norepinephrine and Immunoglobulin Level," Journal of Human Stress 11, no. 2 (1985), 52–59.

M. J. Raleigh and M. T. McGuire, "Social and Environmental Influences on Blood Serotonin Concentrations in Monkeys," Archives of General Psychiatry 41, no. 4 (1984), 405–410; also M. J. Raleigh, M. T. McGuire, et al., "Serotonergic Mechanisms Promote Dominance Acquisition in Adult Male Vervet Monkeys," Brain Research 559, no. 2 (1991), 181–190.

R. Ader and N. Cohen, "Behaviorally Conditioned Immunosuppression and Murine Systemic Lupus Erythematosus," Science 215 (#4539) (1982), 1534–1536.

Robin Casarjian, Forgiveness: A Bold Choice for a Peaceful Heart (New York: Bantam Books, 1992).

Notes:

Record two daily actions you will take to improve each dimension of wellness.

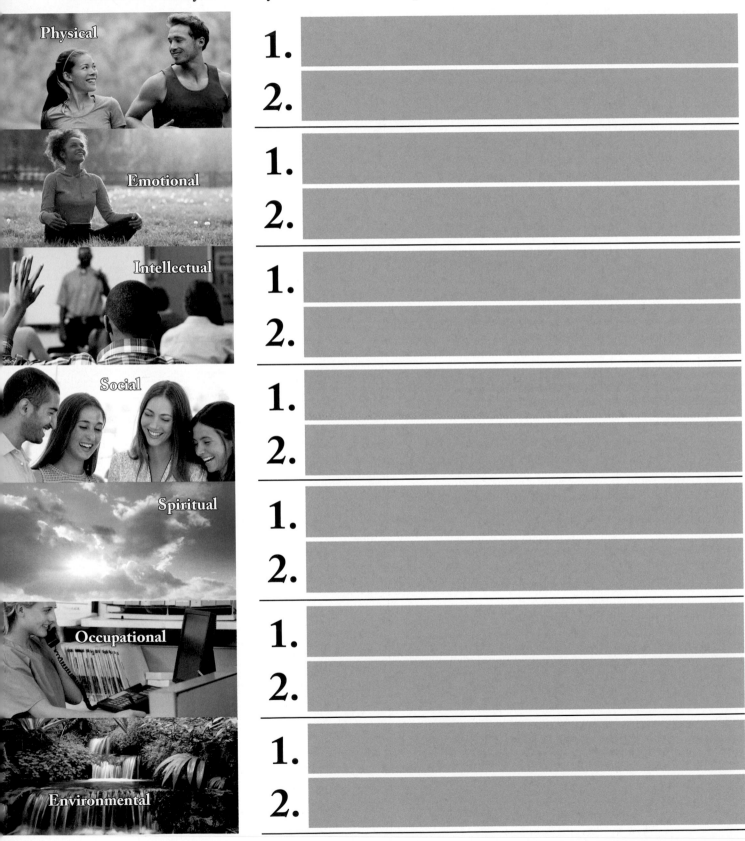

Physical

1.

2.

Emotional

1.

2.

Intellectual

1.

2.

Social

1.

2.

Spiritual

1.

2.

Occupational

1.

2.

Environmental

1.

2.